PROVENCE

A Country Almanac

LOUISA JONES

Photographs by Louisa Jones, Vincent Motte,
Michel Barberousse, Philippe Giraud, and others

Stewart, Tabori & Chang
New York

To Bernard, my countryman

Designed by Adriane Stark
Updated pages designed by Lisa Vaughn

Text copyright © 1999 Louisa Jones
Due to limitations of space, photo credits appear on page 171 and constitute an extension of this page.
Map by Oliver Williams

Published in 1999 by
Stewart, Tabori & Chang
A division of U.S. Media Holdings, Inc.
115 West 18th Street, New York, NY 10011

Distributed in Canada by
General Publishing Company Ltd.
30 Lesmill Road
Don Mills, Ontario, Canada M3B 2T6

Library of Congress Cataloging-in-Publication Data

Jones, Louisa
Provence: a country almanac / Louisa Jones.
p.   cm.
Originally published: New York : Stewart, Tabori & Chang, 1993.
Includes bibliographical references and index.
ISBN 1-55670-862-9 (alk. paper)
1. Provence (France)—Guidebooks. 2. Seasons—France—Provence—Almanacs.
3. Country life—France—Provence—Pictorial works.
4. Provence (France)—Social life and customs—Pictorial works.
I. Title.
DC611.P961J66   1993b
914.4'904839—dc21   98-39754
CIP

Printed in Japan

10 9 8 7 6 5 4 3 2 1
First Printing

Rhône
Nyons
St.-Paul-
les-Trois-Châteaux
Rochegude
Bollène
Vaison-la-Romaine
Suze-la-Rousse
Cairanne
Malancène
Serignan
Bagnole
Crillon-le-Brave
ORANGE
Carpentras
Chateauneuf-du-Pape
VAUCLUSE MTS.
Tavel
Isle-sur-la
Sorgue
Fontaine-de-Vaucluse
Villeneuve
Gard
AVIGNON
Gordes
Apt
Barbantane
Bonnieux
Maillane
LUBERON MTS.
Tarascon
Saint Rémy
ALPILLES MTS.
Durance
Les Baux
Le
Paradou
Lunel
Salon
ARLES
Mausanne
PROVENCE
MONT SAINTE VICTOIRE
Aix-
en-Provence
CAMARGUE
Rhône
Les-Saintes-
Maries-
de-la-Mer
MARSEILLES
Mediterranean Sea

Contents

Printemps

Spring

Eté

Summer

Autumn

92

Winter

132

Introduction

For centuries, country life and lore found expression in the farmer's almanac—a season-by-season guide that provided practical advice, quotations and proverbs, folklore, information about local festivals, recipe suggestions, curious bits of regional history, portraits of famous people, humor and entertainment for leisure moments. Benjamin Franklin created an internationally celebrated best-seller with *Poor Richard's Almanac*, published yearly between 1733 and 1758. Some 150 years later, southern French poet Frédéric Mistral tried to preserve the flavor of old-time Provence in a similar work.

Both Franklin and Mistral followed the usual pattern for almanacs: All items are short, pithy and amusing. Their only logic is that of the seasons, and surprising juxtapositions are part of their appeal. Almanacs aim to delight and instruct, supplying new background material, fresh insights and up-to-date information. *Provence: A Country Almanac* was inspired by this rural tradition. It is not, however, linked to a particular year, and it is designed for a far wider audience.

In recent years, people all over the world have been showing interest in Provençal country ways. The subject has almost become a media cliché. The present volume was not written, however, in response to a current fad; rather, it grew out of 20 years' experience teaching Provençal culture to American students in Avignon. Preparing these courses entailed exploring the region's history, geography, literature, arts and crafts, and even gastronomy, as fully as possible. Many portraits of this celebrated area touch only the surface; but its justifiably famous traditions of good living still hold many happy surprises, both delight and instruction for interested readers.

One popular misconception about Provence is that it has maintained its rich culture by living apart from the modern world, which is today threatening to spoil it. In fact, the Midi has drawn foreigners for millennia—starting with Greek traders 600 years before Christ. Always a major crossroads, invaded numerous times from the north and from the sea, it has nonetheless maintained its own strong identity. Indeed, outside influences have often enriched Provençal culture: For example, the brilliantly ornamental fabrics that are so popular today were originally printed on cottons imported from India; and salt cod, the basis of many a local dish in the remoter, inland areas, sometimes came all the way from New England. Even in the remote Middle Ages, small Provençal cities maintained active trade with distant places, thus bringing new wealth to a landed gentry whose rich valley farms later housed whole communities. The elegant way of life of this class, which reached its peak in the mid-nineteenth century, now evokes much nostalgia.

In the age of the European Community, when missile bases are built just steps away from famous truffle markets, can this vision still have meaning? The old ways embodied a certain *savoir vivre,* currently translated as "art of living"; it is this that makes Provence an inspiration for people today in many, far-flung places. At the same time, however, as food writer Leslie Forbes puts it, "The recent spotlight on Provence has had one beneficial result—an increase in regional pride."

Whatever the future may hold, Provence's rich heritage is clearly linked to the land. The town of Saint-Rémy-de-Provence, for example, has been famous for centuries for its spring vegetable market. Now it is attracting many jet-set personalities, from rock stars to royalty, as a summer retreat. One local woman, a farmer's daughter who is also the descendant of a great poet and the wife of a successful painter, judges that her community still has about an equal number of working farms and cosmopolitan vacation homes. As long as that proportion can be maintained, she believes, the old values can survive.

Max-Phillipe Delavouet, another southern poet (one of many), concludes that "art in Provence, in its best manifestations, is always peasant art. It never forgets the earth from which it springs and its finest works, even those born in cities, always keep that refined and rustic air which confers nobility on our countryside. . . ."

Provence country life is all about "that refined and rustic air," some of which, I hope, has found its way into these pages.

Louisa Jones
Avignon, 1999
www.enprovence.com

The theatrical unveilings of flowering orchards among

 the silver and somber greens of olive and

cypress: almonds followed by apricots and

plums, cherries, peaches, apples, pears and quinces.

Fires among the fruit trees for frost protection. Small

Spring in

lambs and kids taking their first stumbling steps in

open fields and, within the hour, racing around mer-

rily; the shearing of the sheep and their departure for

the summer pastureland of the pre-Alps.

Pounding rains and spring floods . . . and

still frost. Delicate bulbs completing their growth cycle

in preparation for summer dormancy . . .

sheets of wild narcissus and iris on the

hillsides of the Luberon and Mont Ventoux.

The first swallows and then the nightingales. The first

Provence is . . .

of May, considered to be the first day of summer in

Provence. Numerous flower festivals celebrating young

lovers. All the delights of the market gardens: the first

asparagus, strawberries, cherries, melons, apricots.

Pentecost, the first harvest festival.

Spring

*Gardens in Provence mingle aromatics such as fennel, lavender, hyssop and rosemary
with similar perennials (here the yellow swirls of phlomis)
for exuberant scenes where shapes and texture count as much as bloom.*

A Glorious Spring Garden: Giverny in Provence

[Joseph Bayol, Route de Maillane, 13 Saint-Rémy-de-Provence.
Tel: (0) 490 92 11 97. Art gallery open on weekends.]

Spring had really come.
The south opened like a
mouth. It blew one long
breath, humid and warm,
and flowers quivered inside
the seeds, and the round
earth began to ripen like
a fruit.
Jean Giono, REGAIN

Tucked among the lush farms that surround the mar-
ket-gardening center of Saint-Rémy lie many old
properties that now serve other creative purposes.
Indeed, this area supports more artists per square foot
than any other part of provincial France. For many, it is
the landscape that inspires them; but for Joseph Bayol, it is
also the rich garden that his wife tends at their doorstep.

In the late 1960s, the couple bought a property that had
once grown vegetables, a rectangle of about 1,000 square
yards, separated from neighbors, as is customary in this
countryside, by thick cypress hedging. The house they built
on this land is now adorned with traditional trelliswork along
its south side. Here vines and wisteria climb and intermin-
gle. Next door is a small gallery, where Monsieur Bayol's
artistic efforts as well as those of many friends—painters,
sculptors, jewelry makers, furniture designers—are on display. In front of both house and gallery lies the garden.

Cherry trees, planted by former owners, are flanked by a
pink-flowering horse chestnut and three redbuds. Closer to
the house is a persimmon tree, which is draped with golden
fruit in autumn. Paths wind through densely packed flowers—perennials from poppies to delphiniums to Japanese
anemones, and annuals that thrive in the rich soil. Madame
Bayol's columbines are twice the size of any others in the

Painter Joseph Bayol of Saint-
Rémy lovingly paints the gar-
den that his wife cultivates for
his pleasure and inspiration.

ABOVE: *Early, spring-flowering photinia frames the bird-man statue in the garden of the Auberge de Noves near Avignon.* OPPOSITE: *Iris and redbud together enhance the Mas de la Pyramide near Saint-Rémy-de-Provence.*

Alpilles, and her husband loves to paint them.

Such floral abundance suggests an English cottage garden, or the riot of color at Monet's beloved Giverny, more readily than a Mediterranean setting. But farm gardens are also traditional in Provence: Van Gogh admired—and painted—their brilliance in 1888, citing dahlias, pomegranates, figs and red roses.

Monsieur Bayol's paintings capture the strong contrasts of sun and shade, throughout the day and year, that only a Mediterranean climate can produce. Although his work has been exhibited in Paris, Washington and San Francisco and been seen by an ever wider audience, he remains a homebody. He and his wife are deeply rooted in the soil of Saint-Rémy.

The Miracle of Tarascon

This charming small town on the Rhone's left bank was long beset by a water dragon of frightful appearance called a *Tarasque*. Somewhat resembling a giant porcupine, every year it devoured a good proportion of the local young people. Luckily Saint Martha, one of Provence's most popular saints, was able to tame the beast, a miracle that was commemorated for centuries by a public festival in May. A model of the Tarasque was paraded around the town, followed by joyful crowds. As rowdy as Carnival, this holiday used to be considered a failure if no one broke an arm during the day.

If the first four days of April are windy, forty more like them will follow.
Si les quatre premiers jours d'avril sont venteux, il y en aura pour quarante jours.
Si l'abrihando es venousa, n'ia pèr quaranto jour.

Cold in April means bread and wine, but a cold May destroys the harvest.
Avril froid donne pain et vin, si mai est froid, il moissonne tout.
Abrieou fres pan et vin douno, S mai es fres l'y va meissouno.

Among the professional corporations that always took part in the long parade were the Gardeners, mounted on a flower-bedecked float, carrying vases of rare blossoms and herbs. With great delicacy, before the eyes of an admiring public, they planted out a most agreeable garden. A local troubadour, Desanat, quoted by nineteenth-century poet Frédéric Mistral, described what would usually happen next:

The entrance to an elegant manor house in the Alpilles reveals the splendid, carefully pruned canopy of ancient plane trees within.

While the plants line up
And measures are made
Near the girls to court
Three lads start to turn
Then, without warning
Throw into their bosoms
Seeds which tickle . . .
If the beauties allow
While they are scratching
The lads take advantage
And plant a kiss.

But as every good gardener knows, seeds must be watered, and so the gardeners naturally gave the girls—and the laughing crowd—a good soaking with the watering cans. Then a shower of bonbons and bouquets was thrown, and more than once, according to the poet, marriages would follow soon after.

Today, the Fête de la Tarasque has been replaced by a wonderful flower festival, which takes place on Whitsun weekend (late May or early June). Dealers in rare plants display their wares for gardeners who come from far and wide.

L'OURTETO HERB SOUP

▲▲▲▲▲▲▲

The name of this simple herb soup means "little garden." The recipe has been adapted from Réné Jouveau's *La Cuisine provençale de tradition populaire.* Serves 4.

2 pounds fresh spinach
Handful of young celery leaves
1 pound sorrel leaves
1 medium leek, white part and
*   small section of the green*
Salt
1 small onion, sliced
2 cloves garlic, minced
4 thin slices dense country
*   bread*
4 tablespoons olive oil
4 fresh eggs

Wash and drain the spinach, celery, sorrel and leek; coarsely chop each vegetable. Place the vegetables in a pot, cover with water and bring to a boil. Add salt, the onion and garlic. Simmer the mixture for about 30 minutes. Place the slices of bread in a soup tureen (or place a slice in individual soup bowls) and

Manguin Fruit Liqueurs and Brandies

[Jean-Pierre Manguin, Ile de la Barthelasse, 84000 Avignon.
Tel: (0) 490 82 62 29 and (0) 490 86 56 60. Visits by appointment.]

Hidden between two channels of the Rhone, just beyond Avignon's picturesque medieval bridge, lies the Island of Barthelasse—rich vineyards and orchards only minutes from the city center. Down its winding back lanes can be found a number of elaborate old properties, some of which were originally built in the fourteenth century as hunting lodges. One of the most impressive belongs to the Manguin family, producers of fine fruit brandies and liqueurs.

Agricultural engineer Claude Manguin, son of early Fauve painter Henri Manguin, began to farm here during World War II while his father continued to paint in his studio in Avignon. It was not long before Claude decided to specialize in the production of luxury pears and peaches. These choice fresh fruits are now sold in local markets, bearing a dab of red wax on each stem to preserve freshness; they are even more widely appreciated in alcoholic form. Today, grandsons Jean-Pierre and Henri, like many heirs to family businesses in Provence, combine traditional methods requiring a great deal of individual attention with the most modern machinery and techniques. They have also become leaders in the crusade for organic production of fruits and vegetables.

British novelist Ford Madox Ford described the Island of Barthelasse as an earthly paradise. And after a recent visit to the Manguins, U.S. Department of Agriculture specialists had to agree. The soil has been enriched by centuries of flooding, controlled and directed (most of the

sprinkle them generously with the olive oil. When the vegetables are tender, add the eggs to the broth, partially cover the pot and poach the eggs lightly for about 3 minutes. Pour the entire mixture over the bread in the tureen and serve immediately.

time!) by a system of ducts and dikes. Both the poplars bordering the island and the ivy that grows at their feet provide shelter for more than 15 different insects that help to combat fruit pests. The ecological balance in these orchards is indeed harmonious. For example, while most local fruit growers spray their trees three times a year against red-spider mites, the Manguins have not treated theirs in ten years—and in some sections, not for 17 years! The fruit they produce are beautiful to the eye and to the palate . . . and are healthy as well!

Creativity and enterprise are family hallmarks. In the 1940s, when Jean-Pierre was a boy, he wanted to buy one of his grandfather's paintings. First, he cut down a tree to sell for firewood, but the proceeds did not amount to the "family price" of 3,000 francs required to purchase it. To earn the rest, Jean-Pierre patiently grew and sold vegetables. Today, reproductions of Grandpapa's paintings are used to advertise the produce of the estate.

The range of brandies and liqueurs (and related items, such as alcohol-filled candies) has been deliberately limited so that distillation can follow immediately after natural fermentation, in season. (Companies that treat many different fruits often block the first fermentation by the introduction of an acid; this intervention allows distillation to be postponed to a more convenient time.) Best known is the Manguins' *eau de vie de poire,* or white pear alcohol, made from the excellent Williams pear (known in the United States as the Bartlett). Available in bottles of 350 milliliters, 700 milliliters and 1.5 liters, aged a minimum of two years, this brew is smooth and mellow. Grandfather's taste for warm colors and light has found a successful new expression.

Early Fauve artist Henri Manguin painted fruit lovingly; his descendants distill the fruits of Provence into a variety of delicious nectars.

Weatherworn stone statues around the Roman basin at the bucolic Château de Roussan have been listening to nightingales in the nearby thickets for more than two centuries.

Visited by the Nightingale

In the first half of April, one of the Provençal gardener's favorite companions, the nightingale, makes its presence felt. The mellifluous voice of *Luscinia megarhynchos* emerges from thickets and glades ("verdurous glooms and winding mossy ways," says Keats), from marshlands as well as dry areas, on moonlit nights and on cool mornings. Plainly dressed, this bird is a wonder to hear but difficult to see—so much so that the Greeks invented a powerful myth to explain its shyness. They portrayed the nightingale as Philomel, sister-in-law to the king of Thrace who, having done violence to her, cut out her tongue. The gods turned her into the bird, a victory for voice much celebrated by poets, such as T. S. Eliot in *The Waste Land:*

> *The change of Philomel, by the barbarous king*
> *So rudely forced; yet there the nightingale*
> *Filled all the desert with inviolable voice*

Nightingales are less common in the south of France today than they once were. In a description of Tarascon in the 1930s, British novelist Ford Madox Ford remarked that "upon that wall—and at noon—I have known the nightingale voices to be as loud and extended as were those of the starlings on the cornices of the National Gallery." He added that in the heart of town you could not sleep for the abundance of their music.

Southerners often take a less romantic view of the bird than Anglo-Saxon poets, and consider it a nuisance. Transcriptions of its song are hardly appealing: "Jug jug," "chooc, chooc," "a crescendo based on 'pioo,' with many guttural and froglike noises," "hweet," "tacc, tacc," a "scolding 'krr' and a grating 'tchaaa'." Not really a love song, moreover, this virtuosity is intended for the defense of territory!

March wore out its rainy gusts, April its rainbows and May arrived, gently wet, bringing the wild thyme and the sainfoin into flower. Among the beehives one could see, between ten in the morning and noon, huge bursting suns—the first flights of young bees getting their bearings at the home base, a sure sign that the births were continuing on schedule and that the swarms would not be long in emerging.
Marcel Scipion, MEMOIRS OF A BEE SHEPHERD

Still, for John Keats, in his "Ode to a Nightingale," this song conjures up visions of southern wine, "tasting of Flora and the country green, dance, and Provencal song, and sunburnt mirth...." F. Scott Fitzgerald was so moved by these romantic sentiments that when writing about southern French landscapes in *Tender is the Night*, he borrowed his title from Keats's poetic homage to the nocturnal bird.

Luscinia megarhynchos is related to chats, wheatears, thrushes, robins and redstarts. In Provence, one of the latter species, *Phoenicurus phoenicurus*, is also known as a nightingale (*rossignol des murailles*) and is very active and sociable.

Van Gogh's Train Stopped in Avignon

[Fondation Angladon-Dubrujeaud, 5 rue Laboureur, 84000 Avignon. Tel: (0) 490 82 29 03; FAX: (0) 490 85 78 07. Curator: Madame Anne Marie Peylhard. Open afternoons 1 P.M. to 6 P.M. except Mondays and Tuesdays.]

This intimate art and furniture museum is set in the elegant townhouse of two Avignon artists, Jean and Paulette Angladon-Dubrujeaud, who inherited vast collections from Parisian fashion designer Jacques Doucet. These range from medieval to modern art and include the only genuine Van Gogh visible in Provence! Its subject, a moving train, reminds us how fascinated the painter was with modern life. There is also a Cézanne still life, a vivid Modigliani portrait, a jaunty Picasso still life, a haunting Sisley snow scene, and works by Manet, Degas, Foujita and Derain.

LEFT: *Earthenware urns and jars, like this one containing a hosta at the Bayol garden, are for sale at the shop Jardins de Provence. ABOVE: Painted by Vincent Van Gogh in August 1888, this scene of modern life, a train, is the only canvas of the Dutch painter now visible in Provence.*

Food with the Famous in Arles I:
Henry James and
Vincent Van Gogh

Henry James describing the cashier at the café in Arles: "...a large quiet woman who would never see forty again, an intensely feminine type, wonderfully rich and robust and full of a certain physical nobleness. Though she was not really old, she was antique; she was very grave, even a little sad. She had the dignity of a Roman empress, and she handled coppers as if they had been stamped with the head of Caesar."

The Provençal city of Arles has long been famous for its Roman ruins and its dry sausage. For centuries, it was visited by every curious traveler wandering through the South of France. Most arrived by stagecoach and disembarked in the Place du Forum, built on the site of the former Roman market. Henry James stopped here in 1882 and judged the square "ill-proportioned...not at all monumental, and given over to puddles and to shabby cafés." At one end he noted "two shabby old inns which compete closely for your custom." Whichever you chose, he complained, you were bound to wish you had gone to the other. He picked the one that had a fragment of Roman column built into its façade and that, in those days, was called the Hôtel du Nord.

Both this establishment and its rival, the Hôtel du Forum, still exist today—both in considerably better condition than in James's time! The Hôtel du Nord was rebaptized Hôtel Nord-Pinus by the Pinus family, who owned it in the late nineteenth century. Their main contribution seems to have been a name that never ceases to puzzle and amuse patrons. But few hotels in the world can claim to have entertained as many celebrated guests—and few have had the honor of being so roundly condemned, until very recently, for bad food. Each famous traveler records disappointment and goes on to relate how he or she fared better elsewhere in town.

Remembering that Stendhal had also stayed there half a

The purplish flowering of Judas trees or redbuds overlaps the feathery salmon bloom of the tamarisks in a typical rustic scene.

Van Gogh on the women of Arles: "Color plays such a tremendous part in the beauty of the women here. I do not say that their shape is not beautiful, but it is not there that the special charm is found. That lies in the grand lines of the costume, vivid in color and admirably carried, the *tone* of the flesh rather than the shape. But I shall have some trouble before I can do them as I begin to see them. Yet what I am sure of is that to stay here is to go forward. And to make a picture which will be really of the south, it's not enough to have a certain dexterity. It is looking at things for a long time that ripens you and gives you a deeper understanding."

A typical vertical village house in Gordes shelters a private patio garden.

century before him, Henry James wondered if the place should be revered as some sort of relic in spite of gritty floors and dirty window panes. He did not actually dare to eat in the place and fled its *table d'hôte*, sure that he would encounter here, as already in Narbonne, "the dreadful *gras–double*"—greasy tripe. Instead, he sought refuge in one of the cafés of the Place du Forum and there took great pleasure, not in the food, but in looking at the formidable woman presiding at the cash register. The women of Arles were already then famous for their beauty—upswept Provençal chignons and Roman noses. Each traveler in turn, coming to Arles, comments on their imposing presence.

This café might well have been the one just across the street from the Hôtel Nord-Pinus, made famous by another admirer of Arlesian women, Vincent Van Gogh. Being a resolutely modern man, Vincent came to Arles by train. And being poor, he chose a cheap pension near the station. For him, the Hôtel du Nord was neither shabby nor old-fashioned; it was simply beyond his means. But he often drank under a starry sky at the café opposite it, which he immortalized in his painting of *Le Café, le Soir*. Today this establishment is inevitably called the Café Van Gogh.

Van Gogh also had problems with the food in Arles. Arriving in mid-February and in poor health, he longed for meals that would build up his strength. He wrote his brother: "You know, if I could only get really strong soup, it would do me good immediately; it's preposterous, but I never can get what I ask for, even the simplest things…And it's the same everywhere in these little restaurants. But it is not so hard to bake potatoes?" The management of these bistros were not willing to take special orders. Van Gogh realized this, pondering: "One must know the local patios,

Provençal garden fountains appeal to all five senses, blending pleasure with necessity.

and learn to eat bouillabaisse and garlic, then I feel sure one could find an inexpensive, middle-class boarding house...."

Unbeknownst to Van Gogh, a cheerful band of local poets was also looking for authentic Provençal food in Arles. Not being down and out, they started at the Hôtel du Nord. But finding it wanting, they moved on to the sort of working-class dive that would have surely resuscitated the Dutch painter, had he but known where to look. *To be continued...see page 90.*

A Cocktail rose bursts into brilliant spring color against an old castle wall.

A Striking Site: The Open-Air Terrace Museum at Goult

[North of the N100 road from Avignon to Apt, through Lumière, up through the medieval hilltown of Goult, beyond the ramparts, to a small parking lot next to a stone tower (an abandoned windmill). A footpath to the conservatory leads off past the tower and is marked with explanatory panels and arrows. If one walks at a comfortable pace, while admiring views on both sides, it will take about 15 minutes to reach the site.]

Hundreds of miles of terracing still punctuate the steep slopes of Mediterranean France. Their beauty lies not only in the lines they create on the hillside but in their considerable detailing: steps from one level to another, constructed most frequently parallel to the wall itself; tall stones to indicate special passages or ends of vine rows on the outer edge. There is a whole language to the stonework of these landscapes. Unfortunately, intensive farming of the fertile land; a diminished labor force (especially after World War I); the mechanization of agriculture; specific calamities, such as the phylloxera epidemic; and, in general, the rural exodus have all contributed to their abandonment. Dry stone walls are hard to maintain and few people today know how. Some terraces are now used to pasture sheep and goats, whose activity quickly causes walls to deteriorate. And, if the quick drainage of heavy rains is impeded in any way, the walls soon develop "bellies" and give way.

Attempts are now being made to conserve these hillsides for specialized crops. Despite the need for intensive labor, these plants benefit from the terraces' microclimates, deeper soil and resistance to erosion and even fire. Dried flowers, herbs and aromatics; luxury potatoes, such as the famous

OPPOSITE: *Stone huts called* bories *can be found on many terraced hillsides around Gordes, including those of the Open-Air Terrace Museum.* ABOVE: *Hillside terracing involves intricate designs and constructions, such as these upright stones topping a solid wall at the museum.*

ratte beloved by Parisian chefs; Japanese artichokes (*Stachys tuberifera Naud*); kiwis; raspberries and other bush fruits are now being cultivated there. In addition, peach, almond, apricot, fig and olive trees, which have always been grown here, are being irrigated to increase their production. Plantations of other varieties have been added or extended; walnuts and chestnuts on the northern or higher slopes; truffle oaks, pistachios, caper bushes and pomegranates facing south. With the use of solar greenhouses set against the back retaining walls, avocados and Brazilian passionflowers are flourishing.

APARE, a cultural association based in Avignon (41, cours Jean Jaurès, 84000 Avignon, telephone: (0) 490 85 51 15), began the restoration of this village site near Goult in 1982. First, the group organized a workshop similar to others it has set up to preserve various historical monuments reflecting the rural heritage of Provence. One can now see traditional shelters, beehives and cisterns, either made from dry-set stone or dug directly in the rock. And, thanks to the Luberon National Park and the Botanical Conservatory of Porquerolles, a plant museum has been established containing local essences typical of this microclimate: old fruit varieties (notably olive and almonds) that once grew abundantly on such terraces. It is a little-known and strikingly beautiful place to visit.

Soft young grass bending in the breeze, fresh foliage and bloom on fruit trees, new light on old stone and roof tiles—warm spring days in Provence can be a real enchantment.

An April landscape, discovered at dawn from a moving train:

Then, as I watched, the sun rose, and with it the whole panorama ceased looking like an underexposed photograph and came literally to light—the cabin roofs shone orange, the fields turned out to be scattered with poppies the color of new blood, the long green grass was streaked with yellow flowers and cobalt flowers and round scabious flowers that were a hard, firm mauve. Over the distant crimson hills the sky was already blue, and the few people in the fields were a very dark walnut brown. Nothing I had expected of Provence had equaled the harsh and yet mysterious quality of this flying landscape. James Pope-Hennessy, ASPECTS OF PROVENCE

The Fountain of Vaucluse

*[The village and site are east of Avignon, north of the
main N100 road to Apt, near Isle-sur-la-Sorgue, on the D25.]*

y the age of 37, the fourteenth-
century poet Petrarch was the
most famous private citizen
of Europe. He spent his early years in
Avignon, where the Popes then resided,
as did his muse and inspiration, the
divine Laura. But finding public life
oppressive at times, and Laura's presence a source of pain, he took refuge at
the Fountain of Vaucluse, a village that
had enchanted him as a child.

*The emerald water of the
Sorgue flows by the Petrarch
Museum, underneath the castle
ruins that dominate the village
of Fontaine de Vaucluse.*

The actual spring was considered a
natural wonder in Roman times and remains haunting, not only for its dramatic landscape but for its geological
mysteries as well. Indeed, the technical
term "Vauclusian spring" (inverse-
siphon type), which refers to the seep-
age of water through miles and miles
of limestone filters and underground
grottoes to sudden emergence, derives from the Fountain of
Vaucluse. Jacques Cousteau's research teams have been un-
able to plumb its depths: They sent a robot down more than
1,000 feet without touching bottom. The fountain's output
can range from roughly 1,000 to 33,000 gallons per second,
and the temperature remains a constant 53.6 to 55.4° F.

Botanically, too, the site is an enigma. The spring owes its
emerald color to the water parsnip (*Sium officinalis*), which was

Colette, traveling south on the famous "Blue Train" from Paris, describes a Provençal spring:

We just passed Avignon and I might have thought, yesterday, after sleeping only two hours, that I had slept two months: Spring had come to meet me, a fairytale spring, the exuberant, brief, irresistible spring of the South, rich, fresh, with its spurts of sudden greenery, its grasses already high, which sway and ripple in the wind, its mauve Judas trees, its paulownias the color of gray periwinkles, its laburnums, wisteria, and roses. . . . My head has been spinning since Avignon. The northern mists have melted over there, behind the cypress hedges bent by the force of the mistral. The silky murmur of tall reeds came through the open train window that day, along with the scent of honey,

used as a fertilizer for olive trees in the nineteenth century. The moss of the spillway, *Hedwigie acquatica*, is a rare species, growing only in one other valley, near Geneva. Since the output of the spring varies greatly, parts of the spillway are sometimes dry and exposed. At those times, the moss dries up completely, but then turns green again at the slightest rain or increased flow. As for animal life, the river trout are famous, and a few families of beaver still live downstream.

A museum, known as Petrarch's House (his actual house has long since disappeared), is situated across the river from the path leading to the grotto. It contains many portraits of Laura. High above the site stand the ruins of a medieval castle that once belonged to the poet's friend the Bishop of Cavaillon, who would invite Petrarch there to dine. Around the house are several flat spaces, supported by rocky dams, planted out with flowers that beckon colorfully to the pilgrims on the other side. Although not Petrarch's original garden, it nicely evokes the difficulties encountered by the poet in his battle, as he put it, with "the nymphs of the Spring."

In the summer of 1340, Petrarch began to clear a small, stony field with his own hands; he brought in new turf and created a meadow. The nymphs, however, protested by flooding it out and undoing all his work. Undaunted, he started over, but once more a summer storm got the best of him.

After many trials and tribulations, Petrarch tried to make a garden once more. In 1346, he hired peasants, shepherds and fishermen to sink large rocks at the river's edge, forming a breakwater. A stone walk led to a viewpoint, and in the middle of the garden stood a shrine to the Muses. This time it was the winter storms that did the damage to the garden. Petrarch yielded, keeping for himself and the Muses only one rocky nook, strongly fortified.

of pine, of varnished buds, of lilac about to bloom, that bitter smell of lilac before it flowers, a blend of turpentine and almond. The cherry trees cast violet shadows on the reddish earth, already parched with thirst.
Colette, THE VAGABOND

Later generations flocked to the spring because of its romantic associations with Petrarch and Laura, and the fountain became a favorite spot for just-marrieds. When Henry James visited in the 1880s, he remarked on its popularity with honeymooners and "Sunday trippers." James also admired the water's magnificent color and was overwhelmed by its beauty: "You find yourself at the foot of the enormous straight cliff

Early spring rains are much desired in the country. And so it is said that:
April has thirty days /
   If it rained for thirty-
   one / It wouldn't hurt
   a soul.
Avril a trente jours, /
   S'il pleuvait trente
   et un jours / Cela
   ne ferait de mal
   ê personne.
Abriéu es de trento /
   maie quand plourié
   tren'un / Farié mau
   en degun.

out of which the river gushes. It rears itself to an extraordinary height—a huge forehead of bare stone. . . . The little valley, seeing it there, at a bend, stops suddenly and receives in its arms the magical spring. . . . The setting of the phenomenon struck me as so simple and so fine—the vast sad cliff, covered with the afternoon light, still and solid forever, while the liquid element rages and roars at its base—that I had no difficulty in understanding the celebrity of Vaucluse."

Provençal farm domains often have twin-pillared stone entries, as here at Estoublon in the Alpilles.

Here where it is still hilly but not yet mountainous, we have April storms that are as brutal as bulls.
Jean Giono,
RONDEUR DES JOURS

ABOVE: *Village houses sport carefully trained trellises, which leaf out slowly as the season progresses.* RIGHT: *The many-layered geometries of Provençal hilltown design inspired Cézanne, then Picasso and Cubist painters.* OPPOSITE: *The soft tones of climbing roses set off the ocher washes of old buildings. The overhanging tile roof is designed to protect the walls from the infiltration of heavy rains.*

The Muses, from their exile now released,
Share my retreat, but visitors are few
Save those who come to see the famous Fount.
Petrarch, EPISTOLAE METRICA, c. 1340, quoted in
LIFE OF PETRARCH by Ernest Hatch Wilkins

Here I have the Fountain of the Sorgue, a stream that
must be numbered among the fairest and coolest,
remarkable for its crystal waters and its emerald channel.
No other stream is like it; none other is so noted for its
varying moods, now raging like a torrent, now quiet as a
pool. . . . The hills cast a grateful shadow in the morning
and in the evening hours; and at noon many a nook and
corner of the vale gleams in the sunlight. Round about,
the woods lie still and tranquil, woods in which the
tracks of wild animals are far more numerous than those
of men. Everywhere a deep and unbroken stillness, except
for the babbling of running waters, or the lowing of the
oxen browsing lazily among the banks, or the singing of
birds. I would speak of this more at length, were it not
that the rare beauties of this secluded dale have already
become familiar far and wide through my verses.
Petrarch, EPISTOLAE VARIAE XLII, 1347, quoted in
PETRARCH, AN ANTHOLOGY, edited by David Thompson

Skies fill and empty like great sails with the breath of the rogue wind . . . it supples out the cypresses like fur, rushes to explode the spring blossom of almond and plum like a discharge of artillery.
Lawrence Durrell,
MONSIEUR

An ocher-tinted manor house near Apt has a succession of sheltered courtyards.

A Provençal Vegetable Classic: AÏOLI

This feast of fish and a rich array of fresh vegetables can be served at any time of year, with whatever produce is in season—for example, fennel and cauliflower or broccoli can be substituted for tomatoes and zucchini in winter. But to be authentic, it must contain potatoes, chick-peas and the thick garlic sauce that gives the dish its name.

The amount of garlic may seem intimidating, but it is good for the heart and the lungs . . . and there are those who crave *aïoli* as others yearn for chocolate!

Note that the fish must be set to soak two days before the meal, and the chick-peas, the night before.

Serves 6

2 pounds dry codfish	12 cloves garlic, peeled
1 bay leaf	(2 per person is the rule!)
½ pound dry chick-peas	Salt
About 2 cups, plus 1 tablespoon,	Pepper
extra-virgin olive oil	2 cooked beets
Sprigs of fresh thyme or savory	1 celery heart
12 carrots	½ pound fresh mushrooms
12 small potatoes	1 lemon
6 small zucchini	6–12 small tomatoes
½ pound green beans	1 pound of black olives
8 eggs	(optional)

Place the codfish in a large bowl and cover with cold water. Soak the fish for two days, changing the water several times. Remove any bones and skin from the fish and cut into 3-inch squares. Place them in a saucepan and cover with water. Add a bay leaf and poach the fish for about 10 minutes, depending upon thickness. Drain and refrigerate.

Put the chick-peas in a bowl and cover with water. Soak them overnight. Drain, then pour them into a saucepan and cover with water. Add a tablespoon of olive oil and a branch of thyme, and cook for 30 to 40 minutes. Drain and set aside.

Pare the carrots and the potatoes, then clean and trim the zucchini and green beans. Steam the carrots and potatoes for 20 minutes, if winter varieties; for 10 minutes, if young spring ones, adding thyme to the cooking water. Arrange the green beans on top of the carrots and potatoes during the last 5 minutes of steaming, testing until the vegetables are just done. The zucchini take from 5 to 15 minutes to cook and may be steamed with the other vegetables or poached separately.

Hard boil 6 eggs and set aside. Keep the yolks of the remaining two eggs at room temperature, to make a garlic mayonnaise. Using a large mortar and pestle (or a blender or food processor) crush the 12 garlic cloves finely, then add the two yolks and begin to beat the ingredients together. Add the 2 cups of olive oil very slowly, drop by drop, and continue beating. When the emulsion begins to "take," increase the flow of oil to a thin stream. If the mixture should separate, start afresh with another yolk in a clean bowl, adding the curdled mixture gradually. Season to taste with salt and pepper. The sauce should be thick and yellow.

Reheat the cooked codfish briefly.

Peel and slice the beets, cut the celery heart into strips and clean and slice the mushrooms, rubbing them with lemon juice. Arrange all the vegetables, the hard-boiled eggs and the olives attractively around the fish on a large platter. Serve the sauce separately.

Portrait of a Provençal Gardener: Jean Lafont, Rancher

The spring mistral can play havoc with flowerpots on balconies, as here in Sérignan-du-Comtat.

How many gardeners can give advice about which plants best frame a pasture of grazing bulls? Jean Lafont is just such a person, and he has had to consider the question for his own garden in the Rhone delta—that flat marshland, known as the Camargue, which belongs as much to the western province of Languedoc as to Provence. His main activity in life is the raising of bulls on some thousand acres of ranchland, an occupation that combines harmoniously, but surprisingly, with his collector's passion for rare trees and shrubs. Both interests depend on an intimate knowledge of the locality's most unusual microclimate and terrain: The land around the ranch often floods in winter, but can support summer pastures and, closer to the house, a wealth of garden plantings quite unlike those found in the drier hinterland. Monsieur Lafont has decided that olive trees and cypresses would look out of place with bulls behind. Instead, he has chosen stands of tall grasses and reeds, such as tiffa and papyrus, the local tamarisk and cornus, with its bright red stems in winter. The reliable evergreens of the area—cistus, laurustinus, juniper and laurel—are used as hedging throughout the property. His collection, nonetheless, contains 15-odd varieties of cypress in the arboretum in addition to many other rarities. Wooden fences, picturesquely irregular in their double spans, keep the two parts of Monsieur Lafont's life separate.

The rancher owns about 300 bulls, and he knows all of those old enough to fight in the arena by name. He and they will remain friends for many years—for in the Provençal

OLD-FASHIONED SOAPS

[Rampal-Patou, 71, rue Félix-Pyat, 13300 Salon-de-Provence. Tel: (0) 490 56 07 28; FAX: (0) 490 56 52 18. Owner: Monsieur R. Rampal.]

Although soap has been made in Marseilles and the surrounding area since the fourteenth century, it was not until the seventeenth century that the French finance minister, Jean Colbert, turned its manufacture into a model industry. With the arrival of modern detergents, unfortunately, soapmaking went into a decline. Current interest in protecting the environment and ensuring good health, however, have contributed to the growing popularity of Marseilles soap, which is 100 percent biodegradable and good for one's skin. The Rampal family, which has been producing it in Salon since 1910, survived in the 1950s by putting out a line of pure bath soaps containing only vegetable oils (olive, almond, palm or copra) and light washing sodas. It is still popular and is exported worldwide. The washing soap goes through numerous stages—rinsing, cooking, purifying and compressing—before being set out to dry in huge cakes. Later, these are cut into small cubes and stamped with their maker's mark. The smaller versions are individually molded. In addition, verbena, lime and other essences, notably a lavender scent so powerful that a single cake will perfume an entire room, have been successfully added to part of the production line.

course libre, or *course à la cocarde,* the bulls are not killed. The crowd, which knows the animals and is often on their side, watches as each one confronts about 20 young men, who try to remove ribbons (*cocarde*) from the animal's sharp horns. Prize money is offered by local businesses, and the amount increases as the suspense mounts. About 25 such herds, known as *manades,* exist today. Although Jean Lafont's has been in existence since 1851, he did not purchase it until after World War II. The bulls participate in more than a hundred events yearly, one to six animals at a time, and they are treated more like racehorses than are their Spanish cousins. Outsiders are often unaware of the humane way the animals are handled. In fact, some years ago, when the British Queen Mother was to tour Provence, a visit to the Lafont ranch was planned. Her chief of protocol objected, saying that the English public might well misconstrue her appearance there as indicating approval of bull-fighting.

The mid-nineteenth-century ranch buildings reflect the owner's strong personal style. One wall now extends out into a semicircular veranda to let light in during the winter. In the summer, dense shade over this "winter garden" is provided by two ancient plane trees, allowed to soar into the blue. The subtle beiges, grays and greens of their trunks are the dominant tones in the house and the surrounding landscape. Textures play an important role here; they are provided by a wealth of ground covers, under and beyond the planes and other trees, such as the rare *Arbutus andrachne,*

Rancher Jean Lafont has created an unusual arboretum and garden around his farmstead in the northern Camargue. Bulls come and graze just beyond the fence that protects his exotic collection of trees.

with its peeling bark. And there are colorful accents, too. In winter, besides the more common plants, such as forsythia, there are the laurustinus, loquats, shrubby honeysuckle (*Lonicera fragrantissima*), *freylinea cestroides* from South Africa, and a dark green hedge of *saracocca ruscifolia*, with its wonderful scent. A country garden, well-set in its landscape and adjusted to the seasons, but one of great refinement.

Elegance and Intimacy at La Mirande

[La Mirande, Place l'Amirande, 84000 Avignon. Tel: (0) 490 85 93 93; FAX: (0) 490 86 26 85. Director: Monsieur Martin Stein. E-mail: mirande@worldnet.net. Web: www.la-mirande.fr.]

Behind Avignon's famous Papal Palace stands one of Europe's most beautiful hotels, La Mirande. First built in the fourteenth century, it fell victim to fire in 1411, then was remodeled some sixty years later by a prosperous merchant. In 1688 it got its present elegant façade, designed by Avignon architect Pierre Mignard, son of the famous court painter. After the Revolution it was owned by the Pamard family, renowned surgeons. Only in 1987 was it bought from them by an adventurous German family, the Steins, interested in period restoration. The result is a meticulously detailed residence that feels nothing like a museum but everything like a gracious private home—one with nineteen bedrooms and a suite! Parisian decorator François Graf ensured the restoration's professional quality. The interiors now look as if they had been inhabited by a single family since the seventeenth century, with the changes and wear and tear that would normally have

THE CAMARGUE MUSEUM

[Camargue Museum, Mas du Pont de Rousty, 13200 Arles. Tel: (0) 490 97 10 82. Nine miles southwest of Arles on the road to Saintes Maries de la Mer. Open all year except January 1, May 1, and December 25, and Tuesdays in winter.]

On opening in 1979, this vast restored sheepfold received the European Prize for museums. The imaginative exhibits present every aspect of life in the cowboy country of the Camargue, the marshy delta of the Rhône so different from the rest of Provence. Its whitewashed, thatch-roofed

cottages; industries (salt extraction, rice culture, sand wines); wildlife (major bird-migration routes pass over it, and there is a sanctuary in its heart); vegetation (tough, wind-bent tamarisks, and the famous SALADELLE, a wild flower); centuries-old traditions of raising stocky, pearl gray horses and small-scaled, feisty bulls; folklore and festivals, including the biennial pilgrimage to Les-Saintes-Maries-de-la-Mer, for gypsies as well as for the Provençaux . . . all these aspects, along with the region's geology and history, are recounted with the help of slides, reconstructions, illuminated displays, maquettes and models, fine old tools and furniture. Outside one can see the other buildings of this typical ranch and walk on a two-mile trail through the national park in which it lies.

occurred. This approach has allowed inclusion of both an eighteenth-century Salon Chinois and a Napoleon Third Salon Rouge, now the bar. The central courtyard became a delightful glassed-in winter garden. But best of all perhaps is the outdoor terrace and garden, an island of countryside in the heart of the city that ensures that La Mirande remains amazingly quiet even at the height of Avignon's theater festival in July. Occasional house concerts by star performers only enhance the sense of peace.

The Steins first settled in France at Saint-Paul de Vence, where they still maintain an organic garden and keep their own hens— their vegetables, eggs and cut flowers sometimes appear in the dining room. The reasonably priced restaurant achieves high professional standards, however, thanks to chef Daniel Hebet. The Marmiton, La Mirande's cooking school, offers courses by him and other starred chefs, as well as an American and a talented Provençal home cook, Pascale Ferraud.

OPPOSITE: *A charming Renaissance well stands in the courtyard of the Tour Cardinal, near Les Baux.*

RIGHT: *Tucked in behind the Papal Palace in the heart of Avignon, the Hôtel la Mirande's garden remains a haven of peace, even in the summer.*

West Meets West in Provence

Around the turn of the century, a surprising number of exchanges took place between the cowboys (*gardiens*) of the Camargue and their American counterparts—and with several Native Americans. In fact, the decline of the latter group drew much sympathy from Provençal poets such as Alphonse Daudet and Frédéric Mistral, who felt that their own culture was doomed to a similar fate. But it is a Parisian, Joë Hamman, who stands as the key figure in these encounters, which were a mix of life and legend, history, theater and cinema.

Hamman was born into a wealthy Parisian family in 1883.

One of the most spectacular spring flowerings is provided by fragrant shrubby coronillas, here used as a dazzling hedge under the soaring branches of a well-established hackberry tree.

As an adolescent, Joë accompanied his father on a trip to the United States. While there, he happened to strike up a conversation with a factory cleaner, an Indian who had left his reservation. As a result of this chance meeting, Hamman traveled to Montana, where he met the famous chief Red Cloud, now old, blind and in despair. The latter's lieutenant, Spotted Weasel (who was to become the Frenchman's friend for life) gave Hamman his own war costume to take back to France, as well as an Indian name that paid homage to the young man's gentle humor: Mocking bird.

Back in Paris, Hamman later became an actor in the growing movie industry, then a screenplay writer and

I worked [a canvas] to death yesterday, a cherry tree against a blue sky, the young leaf shoots were gold and orange, the clusters of flowers white, and that against the green-blue of the sky made a glorious show. Today alas there's rain, which prevents my going to have another shot at it.
Van Gogh, DEAR THEO

producer. He first went to Provence to play a role in the film version of Mistral's epic poem *Mireille,* and eventually returned to create a whole series of pseudo-American westerns. He invented the character of "Arizona Bill," whom he portrayed in some 200 tales. The hero was famous for his horsemanship, and it is said that at least one Provençal rancher was taught to ride by Hamman, who was active well into his eighties. Hamman also wrote two books, founded a satirical newspaper, and became an expert on Indian affairs. He died in 1974.

Another legendary cowboy, somewhat older than Hamman

The medieval and nineteenth-century battlements of the Château de Barben, near Salon, protect elaborate collections of paintings and furniture which can be visited by the public.

MARIE LEPOITEVIN'S GOAT'S-CHEESE TART

▲▲▲▲▲▲▲▲

When the young kids have been weaned from their mothers, goats' milk is turned into fresh cheeses, which are available in Provençal markets throughout the summer. The filling for this tart can also be used, uncooked, to stuff tomatoes. The recipe serves four as an entrée, two as a light supper dish.

and a native Provençal, was the Marquis Folco de Baroncelli-Javon. Both a friend and a follower of Mistral, he led the life of a gardien in the Camargue (the so-called "Wild West of France") for 60 years while trying to protect its traditions and its threatened minority groups, such as the gypsies. In 1905, he went to Paris to see a popular new entertainment that had just arrived from the United States—Buffalo Bill's Wild West Show. And there he was introduced to Joë Hamman, who served as interpreter for the American Indians accompanying Buffalo Bill Cody.

Thus began a new chapter in the great romance linking Provence and the American West. The traveling show came south, and Baroncelli offered the Indians, Iron Tail and Lone Bear, champagne as they watched a lasso competition between the gardiens of the Camargue and Buffalo Bill's experts. Beaded bags, which the Indians left as gifts for the Marquis, can still be seen in the Provençal folklore museum in Avignon, located in the Baroncelli townhouse.

Frédéric Mistral and Buffalo Bill, who curiously looked much alike, met in Provence. The American offered the poet his dog, and the animal is now buried next to Mistral in the cemetery of Maillane.

All that remains of these friendships are some much-loved relics in museums and private collections. After Hamman's death, his Indian artifacts were handed down to another actor, Jacques Nissou, born in Montmartre and now living in Provence, whom Hamman met in the early 1960s. The younger man certainly shares the elder's sense of the great romance, and, in 1991, made a pilgrimage to the United States to find the tomb of Sitting Bull. As he stood there, thinking of generations of sympathetic exchanges linking the American West and the Camargue, an eagle circled overhead.

Pastry for a 9-inch pie
3 fresh goat's cheeses,
  just barely solid (about
  3 ounces each)
1 tablespoon prepared mustard
Sprinkling of chopped fresh
  chives, parsley or basil
½ cup heavy cream

Preheat the oven to 350° F. Line a pie dish with the pastry.

In a bowl, beat together the goat's cheeses, mustard, chives and cream with a wooden spoon. Pour the cheese mixture into the pie crust and spread evenly. Bake the tart for 45 minutes, with the source of heat from below if possible. (Otherwise, prebake the pastry in a 400° F. oven for 10 minutes before filling.) The filling should be just barely golden color, not brown. The absence of eggs in the mixture preserves the goat's-cheese flavor but prevents the filling from setting like a quiche. Serve the tart with a fresh green salad, preferably seasoned with garlic.

Châteauneuf-du-Pape, Provence's Best-Known Wine

[Paul Coulon et fils, Domaine de Beaurenard, 84230 Châteauneuf-du-Pape. Tel: (0) 490 83 71 79; FAX: (0) 490 83 71 79. Ordering service: (0) 490 83 51 20. Château de Mont-Redon, 84230 Châteauneuf-du-Pape. Tel: (0) 490 83 72 75; FAX: (0) 490 83 77 20. Owners: Messieurs Jean and François Abeille, and Monsieur Fabre.]

Covering some 7,000 acres on the Rhone's left bank, the Châteauneuf-du-Pape wine country produces majestic, full-bodied red wines from an unusual clay soil studded with large, round river pebbles deposited years ago by passing glaciers. Used as mulch, these store heat during the day and increase the grape's sugar, and therefore the alcohol content of the finished product.

The wine's name evokes a fourteenth-century papal castle, now a picturesque ruin overlooking the village of Châteauneuf-du-Pape ("the little town with the big name," says writer Peter Mayle). Pope John XXII constructed this impressive building as a summer residence while living in Avignon. But the vineyards entitled to this controlled appellation label may also belong to the communities of Bédarrides, Courthézon, Orange and Sorgues. In 1923, the vintners of this area founded the first association to set standards for fine wine. And from their efforts emerged the government-controlled rating system used today.

Famous for its varietal mixtures (as many as 13 for one wine; some, like Syrah and le Viognier, were grown by the

In spring begins again the steady, careful nurturing of vines which will produce, if the weather obliges with the right dosage of sun and rain (without hailstones), fine grapes like these.

The vineyards of Châteauneuf-du-Pape are famous for their mulch of large, river-polished pebbles. These store up the heat of the strong Provençal sun and help produce grapes rich in sugar, for wines high in alcoholic content.

Romans); celebrated also for the high degree of alcohol of its wines (up to 15%) and for its small production per acre, Châteauneuf-du-Pape produces wines far better known abroad than a number of its equally deserving neighbors. Many producers offer tastings, in the center of the village or in outlying châteaux.

The Domaine de Beaurenard, belonging to the Coulon family, is located on the southern edge of town, close to the

Avignon road. Both Monsieur and Madame Coulon come from old wine-making families, and their two sons, who represent the seventh generation, are actively involved in the production of Châteauneuf-du-Pape—one trained as a vintner, the other in computer science and business management. Their business is a fascinating mixture of earthiness and sophistication, millennia-old methods of cultivation and the most refined contemporary technology. Madame Coulon

PEACH-LEAF CORDIAL

▲▲▲▲▲▲▲

In Provence, many people make their own aperitif wines from walnuts, oranges and spices, as well as from gentian roots and many other plants. This unusual, fruity version is easy to prepare, provided there is a nearby peach tree.
Makes one quart

120 fresh, young peach leaves
25 sugar cubes
1¼ bottles good-quality wine
  (red, rosé or white)
1 cup white fruit brandy
  (eau de vie) or kirsch

Place the leaves and sugar cubes in a large pan. Add the wine, cover, and either refrigerate or store the mixture in a cool cellar for four or five days. Strain the wine, then add the brandy to it. Bottle the liqueur and cork, but wait at least a week before serving.

explains its operation with obvious pride, her face both weatherworn and elegant, her clothes chosen to resist outdoor exposure and hard work, yet cut in the latest fashion. Throughout the various stages, beginning with the grapes ripening on sunny slopes to their final bottling and labeling, the same piquant contrast between the old and new persists.

This small village cave employs 14 salaried employees and four very hard-working family members. All the processing is done on the premises. The meticulous care needed at every stage is impressive. A sorting of the grapes by quality is obligatory to obtain the Châteauneuf label. At the Domaine de Beaurenard, each person carries two baskets and sorts while picking (the grapes of lesser quality will be turned into Côtes du Rhône). This task requires considerable skill and training—some workers have been harvesting here for 25 years. Although there are producers who do the sorting once the grapes have been delivered to the cave, Madame Coulon believes that there has been too much intermingling by then.

Once the grapes are crushed, they are stored in tall, gleaming, stainless steel vats for 18 to 21 days. The temperature is crucial, for the grapes arrive from the vineyards gorged with sun and need to be cooled. In the old days, they would have been stored underground (at a later stage, longer storage at Beaurenard also takes place some 23 feet below ground level). For the initial period, however, the Coulons have invested in equipment that can be gently cooled (or heated, in a cold year) by water circuits spiraling around the vats. And when the wine has been strained and purified, it moves into a vaulted room, similar to a modern cathedral nave, full of equally immaculate steel vats. The temperature of each vat can be checked immediately at the central computer perched on a balcony above.

Thunder in March means good almonds.
Quant il tonne en mars, l'amande est bonne.
Quan mars tona, l'amendo est bona.

49

For two days now, the wind of the flowers has been blowing, . . . except for the joyful greenery of young wheat fields, the whole countryside is white. The air smells good, trees bend under the weight of this fragrant snow, fallen petals whirl about in the perfumed light like so many white butterflies.
Paul Arène

Flowering almond trees contrast beautifully with dark cypress pillars near the ruins of a Renaissance château north of Aix.

Thus the wines move, under loving supervision, toward their nine-month storage in oak casks. Advanced technology and constant, practical surveillance do not preclude ritual. A collection of wines of the property, some more than 100 years old, is reverently checked every 25 years, before being resealed.

The Coulons have a comfortable and welcoming tasting room, open all year round. In addition, they have opened a fascinating vintners' museum in a nearby village, Rasteau. Their wines (both Châteauneuf-du-Pape and Côtes du Rhône) are imported by most European countries (handled by Grant of Saint James in England and by Park Wines in California), and soon they will also be available on the East Coast of the United States. Unfortunately, the small but delicious production of white Châteauneufs is rarely exported.

In complete contrast to the village cave, the Château-de-Mont-Redon is a country property set to the north of the village, among wild, rolling hills, where the Rhone pebbles among the vines are not only gold but also bleached white. This domain once belonged to the Mathieu family: One famous member was the romantic nineteenth-century poet Anselme Mathieu. Purchased in 1923 by the present family, today the vineyard is run by first cousins, the Abeilles and the Fabres. As with the Coulons, pride and care determine the production of the Mont-Redon wines. Both families have, indeed, won innumerable medals. Mont-Redon wines are imported into the United States by the Kobrand Corporation in New York and are widely available in England at such centers of gastronomy as Harrods and Fortnum and Masons. The family motto, not surprisingly, is "Tradition and Progress."

The sequence of ripening fruits, from cherries and

 apricots to peaches, apples, pears and

grapes. Garlands of garlic and onions hung

on the rafters to dry. Fresh almonds with their furry

green skins. Wheat harvesting and haymaking. Cicadas

Summer in

by day and frogs by night. Swimming pools, siestas,

pastis (the legendary licorice-flavored aperitif). Carry-

ing endless cans of water in spite of

what was supposed to be an automatic

watering system. Examining the sky

anxiously for storm clouds that always bring rain to the next valley, or that ram water into the  ground for just ten minutes, along with hailstones the size of large marbles. For many temperate-climate plants, a second period of

Provence is . . .

dormancy that is similar to hibernation. Forest fires, and still more forest fires. Theater, opera and film festivals. The filtered shade of cool afternoon rooms, of patios under trellises. Dragonflies, praying mantises and grasshoppers.

Summer

Summer living in Provence means dining in cool, refreshing shade, half indoors, half out. Traditional, rustic settings make use of a vine-and-wisteria-laden trellis along the front of the farmhouse. This particularly elegant patio, a separate wing with one wall open onto the garden, adjoins a château.

North of Orange, in front of the nineteenth-century farmstead of scientist and writer Jean-Henri Fabre, a botanical garden displays carefully labeled local plants.

A Great Naturalist's Workshop: The Harmas of Jean-Henri Fabre

[Five miles northeast of Orange on the D976 road to Nyons, just outside Sérignan le Comtat, 84830 Sérignan le Comtat. Tel: (0) 490 70 00 44. Caretaker: Monsieur Pierre Teocchi.]

On the outskirts of a quiet village lies a nineteenth-century farmstead, built by a well-known naturalist of the time, Jean-Henri Fabre, as a haven from the storms of his professional life. Its name, *harmas*, means uncultivated ground, and it proved to be an ideal place for him to observe his beloved insects. The large garden remained wild until after Fabre's death. Since then, it has been transformed into a collection of local plants and wildflowers, all carefully labeled in several languages, but not completely tamed. Visitors can find many corners and paths that have the intense fragrances of the unkempt *garrigue* landscapes.

Fabre's life was a tale of fortitude and perseverance. Born in 1823 to poor café owners, he obtained his education as a scholarship student, but there were long gaps in his studies. He began his first botanical writings in Corsica while teaching mathematics in a high school, and continued them in Avignon after obtaining a teaching position at the Imperial College in 1853. During his tenure there, he became friends with Frédéric Mistral, John Stuart Mill and Stéphane Mallarmé. A popular teacher for 17 years, he, nonetheless, was forced to resign after giving evening classes in natural history: The topic of flower fertilization offended parents of his female students. Jobless, with five children, he accepted a loan from John Stuart Mill that allowed him to settle in Orange and concentrate on writing. Between 1870 and 1879,

Instinctively these days I keep remembering what I have seen of Cézanne, because he has exactly caught the harsh side of Provence. It has become very different from what it was in spring, and yet I certainly have no less love for this countryside burnt up as it begins to be from now on. Everywhere is old gold, bronze-copper, one might say—and this with the green azure of the sky blanched with heat: a delicious color, extraordinarily harmonious, with the blended tones of Delacroix.
Van Gogh, DEAR THEO

he published more than 80 school texts. At the end of this period, he began his famous work, *Souvenirs entomologiques*, which has been reprinted in countless languages. In 1879, he purchased the property in Sérignan.

A traditional Provençal farmstead, the house faces south, but is shaded by ancient plane trees that spread their canopies over the usual terrace and a stone well. A low wall marks the edge of this space, beyond which lies the garden.

Indoors, a small museum displays Fabre's beautiful water-colors of local mushrooms (soon to be reproduced in a special book), editions of his works and samples of his corre-spondence—including a chatty note from Charles Darwin. Upstairs, his study has been maintained intact, with his writing table and parts of his vast collection of fossils, birds' nests, and archaeological artifacts.

Although tended by a devoted caretaker and his family, this site has been somewhat neglected—despite such an enthusiastic fol-lowing in Japan that a plan once evolved to purchase and remove the entire property to the Far East! Local authorities recently agreed that a reception center should be built on nearby land, along with a small museum, so that Fabre's admirers may visit in comfort, without disturbing the tranquillity of the old do-main. More and more people are making the pilgrimage to the home of the man who has often been called the "Homer" or "Virgil" of the insect world. Who better than Fabre illus-trates Virgil's maxim: *Felix qui potuit rerum cotnoscere causae* ("Happy is the man able to penetrate the secrets of nature").

Wheat was once grown much more widely in Provence than it is now. The first harvest, coinciding with the summer solstice, was celebrated by many elaborate festivals and rituals.

In June, the wheat harvest begins, in July it is in full swing.

Au mois de juin on moisonne un peu de blé, au mois de juillet on moisonne à pleines mains.

Au mes de Jun s'en meissouno quaucun, au mes de Juliet se meissouna à plen dèt.

In August, in our region, just before evening, a powerful heat sets the fields ablaze....One could hardly hear the buzzing of a fly drunk on the ray of sunshine that filtered through a crack. Outside the air was burning in columns of fire and, by the threshing floor, between the haystacks, rose up an odor of wheat, fiery as a furnace. The whitewashed, beaten soil radiated against the low wall of the abandoned sheepfold....From there, no noise, not any more than from the barnyard where the animals were dozing....

The heart of the house remained cool, however. ...There remained in this retreat some reserves of shade and freshness that were fed at night and which, during the heat of the day, were a great resource.
Henri Bosco,
LE MAS THÉOTIME

Family Jewels in Grasse

[Museum of Provençal Costumes and Jewels, Hôtel de Clapiers Cabris, 2, rue Jean Ossola, 06130 Grasse. Tel: (0) 493 36 44 65; FAX: (0) 493 36 03 50.]

In an elegant eighteenth-century townhouse in Grasse, Hélène Costa displays her great-grandmother's Provençal dresses and jewelry. As a young girl in Cannes, she once wore some of these costumes when learning Provençal dances. Her collection, extended today, includes everything from the plain dresses of working women to the delicate lace finery of nobility. Some are sewn as "boutis"(appliqué), others as "piqué"(quilting). These examples of exquisite craftsmanship (imaginatively presented by artist Jacqueline Morabito) also give glimpses into how women really lived in earlier centuries—on the farm, in country domains and in town. For example, a foot warmer containing hot coals was once slipped under vast crinolines. This also served in Madame Costa's childhood, to treat head colds—you sprinkled the coals with powdered sugar and inhaled the fumes. One of the finest dresses is the wedding dress of Madame Costa's great-grandmother, who married in 1843 at the age of eighteen. In those days green was the appropriate color for a wedding dress; the tradition for white brides started only after 1860 with the empire of Napoleon III.

The jewelry is presented in elegant eye-level cases, accompanied by evocative photographs. There are examples of the elaborate crosses and cape clasps worn with these dresses, and waist chains given to new brides with the keys of the house by their mothers-in-law, symbolizing their new authority. Hélène Costa's family also owns the Fragonard Perfume Factory next door, open for visits, demonstrations of the perfume-making processes and purchases.

ABOVE: *The "Capucine" cross in the Museum of Provençal Costumes and Jewels in Grasse.* OPPOSITE TOP: *Peach trees flowering in spring provide an almost candy-pink note in the awakening landscape.* OPPOSITE BOTTOM: *An ancient, flower-decked well embellishes the farmstead garden of couturier Bernard Perris.*

Eating figs in the morning is gold, at noon, silver and
   in the evening, lead.
Figues du matin sont de l'or, à midi sont de l'argent,
   et le soir sont de plomb.
Le figo lou matin soun d'or, à miejour soun d'argènt,
   e lou sèr soun de ploumb.

Tavel Wines:
The Château d'Aquéria

[Château d'Aquéria, 30126 Tavel. Tel: (0) 466 50 04 56;
FAX: (0) 466 50 18 46. Owner: Monsieur Paul de Bez.]

LEFT: *On the terrace at the Château d'Aquéria, Anduze jars frame the surrounding countryside.* ABOVE: *The parterre beyond is a green garden in the Italian style.*

Although the rosé wines of Provence have the reputation of being light, summer vacation beverages, best sipped on shaded terraces before siesta time, the Tavel region produces a different rosé, with a wide following and a rich history. The early-eighteenth-century Château d'Aquéria, visible from the Bagnols–Avignon road, sits imposingly among its 130-odd acres of vineyards. A family tradition begun in the 1920s is carried on by two brothers, one who handles the business transactions, the other the winemaking.

They produce Tavel, a dry, full-bodied rosé, from a mixture of Grenache, Cinsault, Clairette, Mourvèdre and Bourboulenc grapes. Before blending, each type is treated separately. Tavel also differs from lesser rosés in its higher alcohol content. So be advised that it packs an unexpected punch on a hot day.

The rosé of Aquéria is consumed all over the world. In fact, a customer once complained that he had to pay more for it at the Carleton Hôtel in Cannes than at New York's Waldorf Astoria. The latter hotel has been a good customer since the 1930s.

Next to Tavel lies the community of Lirac, and at Aquéria one vineyard is split between the two municipalities. Since Lirac also produces fine reds and whites, small amounts of both wines are also available at the château.

A Roman Quarry with Character

[Mas de la Pyramide, quartier Saint-Paul,
13210 Saint-Rémy-de-Provence. Tel: (0) 490 92 00 81.
Open in summer 9 A.M. to 12 P.M., 2 P.M. to 7 P.M. In winter 9 A.M.
to 12 P.M., 2 p.m. to 5 P.M. Owner: Monsieur Mauron.
On the D5 leaving the center of Saint-Rémy towards Les Baux.]

South of Saint-Rémy-de-Provence stand two of the region's finest Roman monuments, which are known as *Les Antiques.* They consist of a cenotaph and a partially destroyed municipal arch. These once indicated the entry to the bustling commercial community of Glanum, whose digs may be visited in the valley nearby. A few hundred yards off lies a former Benedictine monastery, Saint-Paul-de-Mausole, that was converted into a mental hospital in the nineteenth century. It is where Van Gogh spent his last year in Provence. Just behind the cloister, near swaths of lavender that bring out the harmonies of its twelfth-century bell tower, is a parking lot. Here, a sign directs visitors to the most curious site of all.

A small path leads downhill, through a gate, and opens onto a vast oval area, surrounded by low, wooded hills: This spot was quarried by the Romans, who cut out from its slopes the stones used

The ancient quarry of Saint-Rémy-de-Provence, magically lit with snowy cherry trees in spring, will sport intense blue spikes of lavender in summer. An old stone well still supplies the nearby farmstead.

MADAME BOURG'S EGGPLANT MOUSSE

▲▲▲▲▲▲▲▲▲

In his *Almanach*, Frédéric Mistral recounts a dialogue in which Provençaux from different regions compare recipes for eggplant, always so plentiful at the height of summer. In Sérignan, for example, it is stewed in oil, but in Carpentras, it is baked au gratin. In Le Thor, however, it is sautéed with garlic, onion and "love apples" (tomatoes), while in Maillane, it is prepared as fritters. In Saint-Savournin, eggplant slices are dried in the summer sun and served with sausages in winter. In Apt, they are turned into jam! In Pertuis, eggplants are cooked whole in the embers of a wood fire, then opened, salted, peppered and drizzled with olive oil. Some add a crushed anchovy. The following recipe was invented by a cheese seller in the Avignon public market.
Serves 6

to build not only the ancient town of Glanum but also most of the monuments in Arles. A tall, irregular stone column in its center marks the original height of the land before excavation; its apex corresponds still to the level of the surrounding hills. This strange ruin was mistakenly called a pyramid in medieval times—hence the name of the site.

Today, a cherry orchard fills one end of the former quarry, while lavender fields extend around an ancient stone well at the other. And built into the northern slopes is a troglodyte farmstead—the Mas de la Pyramide.

The present owner, Monsieur Mauron, claims his ancestors have lived here since the days of Charlemagne. He conducts tours of both the quarry caves and his house. In the former, he has arranged an impressive display of old agricultural equipment. There are also huge stone Roman vats for storage of provisions, an aqueduct fragment and a wall that slaves scraped at to make gravel for roadbeds. Within the house, rustic furniture (some made from stone) and faded family photographs are grouped as they must have been in the late nineteenth century. Monsieur Mauron lives very simply: In his kitchen, a few potatoes are kept in an earthenware bowl; outside, his dishes are laid out on a slab of rock to dry. At one end of the property, however, he has installed two comfortable guest rooms that may be rented by tourists.

In front of the farmstead, lilacs and redbuds bloom in the spring along with irises that edge the path—very like those painted by Van Gogh, a stone's throw away. The site has unusual character, much like its owner, who lives here happily with his dogs and cats and pet rook, welcoming all those who are interested in the place's unusual beauty and strange history.

3 shallots or mild onions, chopped fine
3 tablespoons olive oil
3 pounds eggplant, peeled and diced
Salt
Pepper
2 cloves garlic, chopped
2 tablespoons chopped parsley (and basil, if you wish)
7 large eggs
2 cups fresh tomato sauce

Preheat the oven to 350° F. In a large skillet, sauté the shallots in the olive oil until they are translucent. Add the eggplant and cook until tender, over very low heat, turning often. Halfway through the cooking, add salt, pepper, garlic and herbs. Put the mixture in a food processor or blender, and purée, or put it through a sieve. In a separate bowl, beat the eggs, then add them to the eggplant mixture. Pour the eggplant mixture into a 2-quart greased loaf pan set in a pan of hot water, and bake for about an hour. Serve the mousse hot or lukewarm with the tomato sauce.

Saint John's Day: Herbal Lore of the Summer Solstice

An olive for Saint John
(June 24), thousands
more to come.
*Une olive déjà pour la
Saint-Jean, mille pour
tous les autres.
Une óulivo pèr Sant-Jan,
milo pèr touti li Sant.*

Medieval land rotation was triennial in northern France, biennial in the south, where milder winters made autumn sowing possible. The wheat was then ready for the following summer solstice, associated with Saint John's Day (June 24), and celebrated as a harvest festival. In the valleys, extra hands were needed from May onward, and workers would come from the northern hills in teams of three—two men cut and a woman collected. Starting in the vicinity of Arles, they would follow the ripening fields north as the season progressed, moving across the land like a tide, arriving home just in time to harvest their own crops.

Around this major event of the agricultural year, ancient pagan rituals became linked to Christian symbolism. Its popular folklore came to permeate the smallest details of everyday life. Saint John's Eve was the time for gathering medicinal herbs such as catnip, sage, some thymes, southernwood, hyssop, and wild hypericum, which is more commonly referred to as St.-John's-wort. Some market centers, such as Marseilles, still hold herb fairs in late June. Old-fashioned gardens in which aromatics are grown together with fruit and flowers are often called St. John's gardens.

In Provence, ladybugs are known as "St. John's hens"; early ripening pears and apples are called *poires et pommes de la Saint-Jean.* When someone sneezes, there are Provençaux who still say, "May Saint John make you grow!" Bills used to be due on June 24; it was also the date that farm workers' contracts were established or renewed, until Toussaint, or November 1.

Two plumbers, "rough characters," broke the garden tap, a rather fancy one with a sort of key-shaped handle that could be removed in order to foil marauders. (In the summer, a good deal of water pinching from the neighbor's well is quite fashionable. You wait until your neighbor goes out and then swiftly water your geraniums.)

Lawrence Durrell, SPIRIT OF PLACE

OPPOSITE: *The picturesque village of Le Crestet.* ABOVE: *Aromatics make decorative garden plants in the Luberon.* RIGHT: *Zucchini mixed with roses in a farmer's vegetable garden.*

One afternoon, in the valley of Refresquières, Manon was sitting in the dry grass, watching the yellow carapace of a small prehistoric monster that had planted its claws on a sprig of Queen Anne's Lace. The large insect remained perfectly immobile, but something was happening inside, for suddenly its back split along almost its entire length, and a pale green creature worked hard to extract itself from this prison. It was wrapped in damp, crumpled wings and it climbed slowly and clumsily to the top of the plant, where it stayed motionless in the burning July sun. It was a cicada. Its body turned brown in a matter of minutes, its wings unfolded, grew hard and transparent, like mica veined with gold.
Marcel Pagnol,
MANON OF THE SPRINGS

Fires are lit on hilltops in Provence, as they are all over Europe, to celebrate Saint John's Day. The proverb *Sant Jan fai fue, Sant Pèire l'abro* ("Saint John lights the fire, Saint Peter stokes it") may allude both to this ancient custom and to the growing heat of summer. Southerners also claimed that anyone who could jump over the St. John's fire without getting burned would be protected against fleas for the coming year.

Today, the northern Provençal town of Valréas maintains its own harvest traditions that began five centuries ago: On the evening of June 23, a five-year-old boy is crowned king for a year and draped in a white sheepskin. He is carried triumphantly through the charming village, accompanied by a torchlight procession of 300 people in period dress, as bowsmen and pages, soldiers and herders with carts of oxen.

Harvest festivities take place in other towns throughout the summer: Some communities celebrate Saint Eloi (June 25), patron of blacksmiths and protector of all farm animals and agriculture. And every village in the northern Alpilles, for example, has a parade featuring a harvest cart, heavily laden with produce and flowers, pulled by about twenty horses decked out with multicolored ribbons, pompons and feathers. Saint Roch merits similar homage. Many of these celebrations are further enhanced by competitions of lawn bowling (*boules*), mass banquets outdoors (usually involving huge quantities of *aïoli*), and Provençal bull running. Often, there is folk and street dancing, which is prolonged late into the evening, accompanied by fireworks. Barbantane, Eyragues, Châteaurenard, Rognonas and Maillane are among the villages holding such festivals.

A Mountain Inn: Crillon-le-Brave

[Hostellerie de Crillon-le-Brave, place de l'Eglise, 84410 Crillon-le-Brave. Tel: (0) 490 65 61 61; FAX (0) 490 65 62 86. Owners: Peter Chittick and Craig Miller. E-mail: crillonbrave@relaischateaux.fr. Web: www.crillonlebrave.com.]

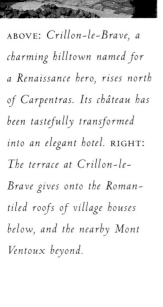

ABOVE: *Crillon-le-Brave, a charming hilltown named for a Renaissance hero, rises north of Carpentras. Its château has been tastefully transformed into an elegant hotel.* RIGHT: *The terrace at Crillon-le-Brave gives onto the Roman-tiled roofs of village houses below, and the nearby Mont Ventoux beyond.*

American novelist Edith Wharton remembers driving into northern Provence: "Ahead of us, all the way from Avignon to Orange, the Mont Ventoux lifted into the pure light its denuded flanks and wrinkled silvery-lilac summit. But at Orange we turned about its base, and bore away north-eastward through a broken country rimmed with hills. . . . " Today, she might have been heading for the Hostellerie de Crillon-le-Brave, a country inn closer to Carpentras than Orange, in a picturesque hilltown named after a Renaissance hero, whose statue stands in the village square. Peter Chittick, an enterprising Canadian, has converted the town's medieval château into a comfortable and elegant hotel. Its bright cotton fabrics and ocher-colored walls; its welcoming sitting rooms furnished with antiques and splendid books about Provence; its chamber-music concerts and chatty newsletter, with tips on local sites and crafts; its terraced garden, where the swimming pool affords a spectacular view of the valley below—all these features lead its many regular guests to consider it as a second home rather than a hotel. Others come mainly to eat local specialties . . . in the garden.

August rain gives oil
and wine.
Pluie d'août donne de
l'huile et du vin.
Pluio d'aous douno
d'ooulivo eme de mous.

Crillon-le-Brave's Olive Mousse

Serves 4

1¼ cups medium-sized black olives
   (preferably Nyons)
1¼ cups heavy cream
½ teaspoon powdered (unflavored) gelatin
1 tablespoon finely chopped chervil
Salt
Pepper
¼ pound fresh escarole, washed and dried
1 tablespoon balsamic vinegar
1 shallot, chopped fine
4 tablespoons good-quality olive oil

Pit the olives, setting aside four halves for garnish. Chop the rest to a fine texture, or purée it in a food processor or blender.

In a saucepan, gently heat ¼ cup of cream, then sprinkle the gelatin over it. Stir the mixture until the granules are completely dissolved. In a bowl, whip the remaining cream, fold in the olive pulp, then the gelatin mixture. Add the chervil, salt and pepper. Pour the mixture gently into four individual molds and refrigerate for at least two hours.

Dip the bottom of each mold very quickly into hot water and unmold each onto individual plates. Place half an olive in the center of each mousse. Surround with escarole leaves.

Pour the vinegar in a bowl and season with salt and pepper. Add the finely chopped shallot, then beat in the olive oil until well blended. Dribble the dressing over the salad and serve.

One after one the Rhone bestowed upon us its historic sites and little drunken towns, snuggled among vines, bathed in the insouciance of drowsy days and drowsy silences broken only by the snip-snop of the secateurs among the vines—the holy circumcision that ends the elegiac summers of Provence.
Lawrence Durrell, LIVIA

The Cuckoo and the Cicada

A popular fable taken from Frédéric Mistral's *Almanach* of 1890.

Now one day the Cuckoo, well-fed and fat, observed while calling "Cuckoo! cuckoo!" that the meadows that year were thickly grown; and that for the May mowing, the local farm workers were making good money . . . and believe it or not, he hired out to mow. And to collect the hay, he took on the Cicada.

But the Cuckoo is an idler, so much so as you know that he lays his eggs in the nests of others . . . and when the summer heat struck, this lazy creature stopped all the time to sharpen his scythe, yawning in the face of the hard work to be done. But the Cicada, thin and light, thrived on the heat and sang out to him petulantly, "Cut! cut! cut! cut!" Then the Cuckoo began again; but after only a few steps, dropped his scythe once more to go have a drink, while the hardworking Cicada exclaimed, "Fat loafer!" and cried, "Cut! cut! cut! cut!" And thus the Cicada continued the livelong day, always scolding the Cuckoo, telling him constantly to cut, cut, cut. . . .

So much so that the plump bird, when the great heat came which ripens the wheat, could stand it no longer and, from laziness, found himself a clump of grass, lay down and stayed silent.

But the good Cicada, gladdened by the sun, hired out to bind the sheaves of the harvesters who were cutting the wheat, and all during the harvest, as long as it lasted, she cried out, "Cut! cut! cut!"

This is why in May, the Cuckoo can be heard, but as soon as it gets hot, he hides and keeps still, while the Cicada sings loud. . . .

The cicada, known as *cigale* in French, is frequently misnamed "grasshopper" in English. In La Fontaine's famous fable *Le Cigale et le fourmi*, it is the cicada who is lazy, dancing away the summer while the industrious ant stores up food for winter. Mistral's Provençal tale, which also contrasts laziness with hard work, portrays the cicada as a hard-working farm woman whose man lets her down.

The poet John Keats also admired the insect's summer song (he also used the term "grasshopper"). In his Romantic English version, however, no one works at all! Just as in the Provençal fable, however, the birds dislike the heat of summer:

> When all the birds are faint with the hot sun,
> And hide in cooling trees, a voice will run
> From hedge to hedge about the new-mown mead;
> That is the Grasshopper's——he takes the lead
> In summer luxury,——and he has never done
> With his delights; for when tired out with fun
> He rests at ease beneath some pleasant weed.

For Keats, both the cicada's summer song and that of the cricket on the hearth in winter simply show that "the poetry of earth is never dead."

Celebrated in antiquity as a symbol of music, the cicada remains a special favorite in Provence today. Ceramic effigies of this creature can be purchased in most souvenir shops.

Olive-Wood Crafts

[A. Parodi et famille. The shop is on the main street of Mirabel-aux-Baronnies, between Vaison-la-Romaine and Nyons, northeast of Avignon on the D938. Tel: (0) 475 27 12 07. Open: 9:00 A.M. to 12 P.M.; 2:00 P.M. to 6:00 P.M., every day but Sunday.]

On display here are many different objects made from elegantly veined hard olive wood. Among them are classic salad bowls as well as mortars and pestles, which are used in the preparation of many traditional Provençal dishes, such as aïoli, or the "rouille" that accompanies bouillabaisse. Since the hard April frosts of 1956 that destroyed so many old orchards, craftsmen have also had olive tree roots at their disposal. Many of these gnarled forms have been transformed into original lamps bases. The Parodis' work can also be found in shops all over Provence, but it is worth seeing at the source, in the heart of the rich olive country around Nyons. Their workshops are situated a mile from the town center and can also be visited.

BELOW: *Oleaders provide color all summer in Provençal gardens.* OPPOSITE: *Orchards of century-old olive trees have an imposing presence. Besides the bounty of their fruit and oil, they provide a dense wood much prized for both carving and burning.*

Terence Conran's Provence Country Home

Celebrated designer and long-standing Francophile, founder first of the Habitat chain and more recently of the Conran Shops, Sir Terence Conran loves his country home in the southern Alpilles. The painter Francis Bacon told him about a house for sale near Aix, but it needed too much upkeep, Conran felt. Discouraged, over drinks with friends he

ROGER VERGÉ'S COOL SUMMER SALAD

▲▲▲▲▲▲▲▲

Serves 4

20 medium-sized black olives
  (preferably Nyons)

2 lemons

3 young, very fresh zucchini
  (no more than an inch
  in diameter)

3 tomatoes, still a bit green

Sea salt

4 sprigs coriander,
  chopped finely

20 fresh mint leaves,
  chopped finely

4 tablespoons good-quality
  olive oil

Pit the olives. In a salad bowl, squeeze the juice of one lemon. Peel the other lemon, cut it into quarters and add them to the bowl. Wash and trim off the ends of the zucchini. Slice the zucchini thinly and add them to the bowl.

Wash the tomatoes and remove the stem ends. Cut the tomatoes in half cross-wise, then cut them into ½-inch cubes. Add them to the bowl. Sprinkle the vegetables with sea salt

met the Demery family, creators of the fashionable Souleiado fabrics. Jean-Pierre Demery recognized in Conran an exceptional creator and innovator and a man of taste. He proposed to show him "the finest farmstead in Provence." Several buyers were interested, but the local agricultural union, which has an important say in such decisions, recommended Conran because he alone would allow the tenant farmer to keep working on his land.

For Conran, the south evokes "sun, the sea, lively and also washed-out colors; an abundance of fruit, vegetables, and flowers; intense aromatic flavors; olive oil, bouillabaisse, and a way of life which is based on simplicity." His particular corner has relatively few tourists and the all-important Canal de Provence, providing irrigation for the patchwork of cypress-hedged fields that produce those succulent flavors and aromas. Conran's property lies just south of this canal, invisible at the top of a hill on its northern boundary. His immense farmhouse, a central building flanked by two low wings, may be of Tuscan inspiration. Its foundations are possibly those of a former Roman villa. Its distinction is confirmed by the majestic lane of horse chestnuts that approaches it from the south.

The main garden has been designed on the north slope, which is cooler in summer, leading up to the canal. A broad esplanade of steps leads up from the patio, with its elegant rectangular basin, to the swimming pool above. Water links the two in the cascades that accompany these steps on either side, not always visible but always audible. Huge terra-cotta urns punctuate the landings, with well-grouped masses of wisteria and canopies of albizzia (sometimes called summer mimosa) trees.

The garden spreads out on all sides, on terraced levels supported by stone walls. A profusion of plantings provides color at all seasons, not least the silvery gray of an olive grove blended with the light russet foliage of *Rosa rubinifolia*. Catnip, irises and rock-

and let them macerate for 20 minutes.

Add the olives and the herbs. Sprinkle with olive oil and toss. Serve immediately, so that the tomatoes and zucchini do not get mushy.

Reprinted with permission from *Les Legumes de Mon Moulin*, by Roger Vergé, published by Editions Flammarion in 1992. Translated by Louisa Jones.

The ocher-toned farmhouse owned by Sir Terence Conran in Provence may have Roman foundations.

roses blend with Russian sage and lavateras on various levels. Lavender intermingles with sage-leafed cistus and yellow flowering phlomis against the deep burnt-orange house walls. Two other rectangles on the hillside have been flattened and paved and planted with plane trees for shade, to provide relaxation areas for lawn bowls and other games.

Conran feels that this plan was partly inspired by the garden of his Georgian house in England. The garden is strong and personal, laid out for summer leisure and pleasure as well as for architectural interest. There is much attention to detail here, and even the outlying areas, left wilder, are full of interesting corners, beds of wild thyme and other aromatics.

In his book *Terence Conran's France*, the designer judges that this corner of the southern Alpilles sums up all the charm of Provence—flavors and savors, colors and smells, an ideal "ratatouille"of the best of country life in this region.

The Conran garden features summer bloom in bright colors for vacation enjoyment.

Authentic Traditional Fabrics: The Olivades

[Les Olivades, Chemin des Indienneurs,
13103 Saint-Etienne-du-Grès. Tel: (0) 490 49 19 19;
FAX: (0) 490 49 19 20. E-mail: les-olivades@provence-fabrics.com.
Visits by appointment only.]

The inimitable designs of Provençal fabrics were first inspired by Indian cottons in the eighteenth century. Now several companies produce them, each with its own style.

Provençal fabrics with their intricate designs and compelling colors have become much more fashionable in recent years. But their popularity dates back to the Renaissance when the Compagnie des Indes began importing printed cottons from India. By the second half of the seventeenth century, local workshops that produced imitations of these successful imports had sprung up all over Europe. As a result, from 1686 onward, successive kings of France forbade them entirely. Provence, on the outer edge of this interdiction, became a center of contraband, continuing production on the Papal territories, which included Avignon. One hundred years passed before this prohibition was lifted. It had only served to increase the popularity of these beautiful fabrics.

The ancestor of today's best-known companies was founded near Tarascon following the troubled period of the Revolution. In 1976, cousins within the family branched out to found the Olivades, now the only manufacturer to maintain traditional means of production in Provence. The original business, Souleiado, has achieved wide international recognition and has moved toward brighter, gayer, sunstruck colors. The Olivades still sells most of its production to Provençal customers, and has retained both the subtler tones and printing processes of earlier times (flat frame rather than rotating drums). Indeed, in Saint-Etienne the entire sequence of production is laid out on tables some 75 yards long. The cottons are cleaned and dried, printed one color at a time, steamed for color fastness, cleaned and dried again, and finally stretched. All of these steps take place in one large building, where about 20 people are employed.

Although the making of these "Indian" fabrics has been a major industry in Provence for centuries, involving many families and whole towns, there has invariably been a highly cosmopolitan dimension to it. For instance, the cottons have always been imported from Louisiana or Calcutta, even in the seventeenth century. Jean-François Boudin, in partnership with his brother and sister, runs the Olivades business. According to him, what characterizes the Provençal style today is the manner of interpreting certain traditional patterns, such as the geometric, nonspecific floral designs, the cashmere swirl, the Imperial bee from Napoleonic times, and the Pompadour bouquet. His generation is the first to have learned English rather than the local Provençal dialect.

Tradition and innovation: Century-old models serve as inspirations for the latest fashions. About 20 percent of the Olivades' fabrics are newly designed every year, in line with current trends. They are sold both as yard goods and ready-to-wear items. The Olivades factory lies among some of the loveliest countryside of the Alpilles, and the patterns seem like a concentration of the subtle beauties of this landscape. The fabrics can easily be slipped onto a patio table, transformed into cushions for a chaise-longue or turned into curtains, shirts or headscarves. (The California company

Summer pleasures in Provence require a careful balance of sun and shade throughout the day.

ZUCCHINI FANS

Serves 4

4 *medium zucchini, washed and trimmed*
4 *medium tomatoes*
2 *tablespoons chopped parsley*
3 *tablespoons grated Swiss cheese*
Salt
Pepper
2 *tablespoons olive oil*

Preheat oven to 375° F. Steam or poach the zucchini for 5 to 7 minutes, or until just barely cooked but still quite firm. Create fans by making two lengthwise cuts almost to the end of each zucchini. Cut the tomatoes into slices and insert them between the layers of zucchini.

Grease a baking dish just large enough to hold the vegetables, and then arrange them gently in it. Sprinkle with parsley, grated cheese, salt, pepper and olive oil. Bake for 15 to 20 minutes, or until lightly browned.

Smith and Hawkins has already made all these adaptations).
They also nicely lend themselves to a variety of decors
and clothing styles. Bags and *pochettes*, fabric-covered boxes,
umbrellas, even bracelets are also available in the company's
shops, which can be found in every town in Provence.

ABOVE: *Lotus seed pods,
emerging from a fountain,
surround a particularly
elaborate terra-cotta garden
ornament.* RIGHT: *The hilltown
of Roussillon is famous for its
ocher quarries. Its houses all
sport tones of orange, flame
and yellow.*

There are gardens of
beans, orchards with
apples, pears and peaches,
cherry trees that catch
your eye, fig trees that
offer you their ripe figs,
round-bellied melons that
beg to be eaten, and beautiful vines with bunches
of golden grapes—ah,
I can almost see them!
THE MEMOIRS OF
FRÉDÉRIC MISTRAL,
trans. George Wickes

*The custom of planting fruit
trees among vineyards dates
from Roman times. Shade trees
in cultivated fields provide a
place to rest and store the
water gourd while working in
hot weather.*

Field Patterns in Provence

Historians of rural France love to discuss the lay-
out of its cultivated fields in an attempt to
explain why there are such radical regional variations, especially between north and south. The hedged
and stone-walled patchwork of the northwest and the long,
narrow "open-field" system of the northeast both stand in
striking contrast to the Mediterranean design. It is thought
that some of these differences are the result of two separate, prehistoric migrations by nomads, one from the
Danube valley and the other from the inland sea, who
moved into the territory that is now France.

It was the Romans, however, who gave the southern
countryside its modern gridlike configuration. They sur-
veyed the entire region and cut it into squares of land that
they called "centuries." Some 415 stone fragments recording
the results of their planning, the oldest dating from about
77 B.C., can be seen in the municipal museum in Orange.
When whole, each of these tablets measured at least 23 feet
by 20 feet; they were all meant to be posted for public
viewing. Thus the Romans, through this division of land
called "centuriation," created a grid pattern for the rural
landscape comparable to the typical Roman town plan, fix-
ing dimensions of holdings at about 375 square feet, a size
still surprisingly common today. In addition, southern
fields also remained small because of Roman inheritance
laws, which gave equal shares to each son rather than the
whole estate to the eldest. It has also been said that southern plowmen appreciated square fields because the water
gourd that waited at the end of each row of plantings could
be reached that much more quickly! However that may be,

THE MIDSUMMER GARLIC FAIR IN MARSEILLES

It hangs in short braids, or loops in long heavy cables from all the stands that spring up in a few hours. It spills from the backs of parked trucks and wagons. It lies in piles on canvas spread on the sidewalks, and there are nutlike sacks of it as tall as a man. Housewives pinch and sniff and fill their baskets for storage; buyers for big hotels and restaurants in Provence sample freely as they make out their orders; wholesalers from half of Europe compare lots and bargain with the farmers. It is exciting, and a handsome scene, with the silky glistening garlic everywhere, to look at and to breathe. Some men in Provence say their women are beautiful because of garlic, and some women

aerial photographs confirm the persistence of this type of Roman patterning in today's countryside.

Another factor that helped determine the country's field patterns was the tool chosen to work the land. Since Roman times, southern fields were tilled with the *araire*, an instrument that differed radically from the northern plow, or *charrue*. The latter, much heavier, needed a team of animals to pull it and hence more turning room at the end of each row. It worked well, therefore, in larger, more regular spaces. The lighter araire, on the other hand, opened the earth without turning it over, and suited sandy, stony soil. It was easier to manipulate on slopes and could be drawn by one animal. The farmer who used it had to plow each field twice, once up and down and once crosswise, to prepare it for sowing. (Many of these araires are on display in country museums today, at the Mas de la Pyramide in Saint-Rémy, for example, and at the wine cooperative in Laudun, near Avignon).

The southern rural landscape is also characterized by its absence of walls between fields. Once again, it is the Romans who are responsible for this. The force of the Roman legal code was such that physical barriers were not necessary to mark the limits of private property. The general survey and a few stones, even clods of earth, sufficed to demarcate holdings. Walls in the traditional Provençal countryside support earth or mark bridges and canals. Both walls and hedges are becoming more common in the modern countryside, however. Although rights of passage for sheep and goats still form part of many property deeds, vacation and retirement home owners have now enclosed large tracts of rural land.

say their babies are healthy because of it, and their men stronger than other men.

M. F. K. Fisher,
TWO TOWNS IN PROVENCE

The Romans loved trees in groves, which had sacred significance in their gardens. Often, they planted these wooded clusters in the middle of fields. Thus began another ancient custom in Provence that was to last for 2,000 years and that was to leave its mark on the rural scenery: the mingling of fruit trees, vines and cultivated strips, called *ouillères*. Typically, three to five yards of wheat would

The intricate Provençal patchwork of agricultural and grazing land changes character from season to season, each with its own colors, textures and light.

be cultivated with four or five vine rows on each side, among which, in turn, stood olive or fruit trees. If modern mechanical and specialized farming has made this mixture impractical, there are vestiges of it everywhere. Even now, it is not unusual to find trees standing in the middle of many fields, providing fruit, or shade when it is time to quench one's thirst from the water gourd.

An Elegant Country Retreat: Le Prieuré

[7, place du Chapitre, 30400 Villeneuve-lez-Avignon,
across the Rhône from Avignon. Tel: (0) 490 15 90 15;
FAX: (0) 490 25 45 39. E-mail: leprieure@avignon.pacwan.net.
Owners: Madame Marie-France Mille and Monsieur François Mille.]

ABOVE: *Rough-hewn stone wells often turn into planters for heat-loving flowers as here, in a garden in Fontvieille.* OPPOSITE: *The colorful gardens of the Prieuré hotel in Villeneuve combine the traditional lines of box-edged parterres with a riot of summer color—a careful blending of annual and perennial bloom.* FOLLOWING PAGE: *Monkfish cocoons, in a simple, olive oil–based dressing, provide rustic but refined fare, here enhanced by old-fashioned Provençal pottery.*

In 1322, Cardinal Arnaud de Via, nephew of reigning Avignon Pope Jean XXII, built a fine residence in Villeneuve. Feeling the approach of death, he set up a priory with a chapter of 12 canons, 12 priests and two deacons, ruled over by a dean, to pray for his soul. Part of this original property became Villeneuve's parish church, and the rest became a private residence. First transformed into a comfortable modern hotel by the late Monsieur Mille's parents in the 1930s, renovated again in recent years, it is one of Provence's "best addresses" for both restful stays and good food. In summer, a formal garden edged with an ancient pergola brims over with colorful blooms, visible from the dining terrace. Chef Serge Chenet has been using a wide variety of local ingredients since 1988. Light, sweet olive oil seasons many of the most refined dishes. Vegetables served here come largely from the plots of nearby neighbors, located beyond the tennis court and the cutting garden, from which Madame Mille collects fresh flowers to make up bouquets for the dining tables.

Monkfish Cocoons with Eggplant

Serves 4

1 monkfish, weighing 3½ pounds

3 medium-sized eggplants

1½ cups extra-virgin olive oil (first cold pressing)

4 ripe tomatoes

1 shallot

1 clove garlic

Salt

Pepper

2 anchovy fillets in oil

SAUCE

1 hard-boiled egg

1 lemon

1 tablespoon salmon roe

½ tablespoon lumpfish caviar

2 tablespoons chopped chives

1 tablespoon chopped parsley

Preheat the oven to 350° F. Grease a baking pan or cookie sheet.

Clean the fish and remove the fillets. Refrigerate them.

Halve the eggplants lengthwise. Make several slits in the flesh with a knife and place the halves, cut side up, in a baking dish. Salt them lightly and drizzle 1 tablespoon of olive oil over them. Bake for about 35 minutes, or until just soft.

Plunge the tomatoes into boiling water for 30 seconds, then peel them. Cut each tomato in half, squeeze gently to remove the seeds and chop the flesh into small cubes. Reserve half for the garnish.

Mince the shallot and the garlic. In a frying pan, heat 1 tablespoon of the olive oil. Add the shallot and cook, without browning, until soft. Add the garlic, then the cubed tomatoes. Season with salt and pepper, and simmer the mixture for 5 minutes, or until soft.

Remove the eggplants from the oven and spoon out the pulp. Chop it coarsely. Heat another tablespoon of olive oil in a large saucepan and add the anchovy fillet. Add the eggplant pulp and the tomato mixture. Simmer, uncovered, until the mixture is reduced. Add more salt and pepper, if necessary.

Prepare the monkfish: Cut each fillet crosswise into 20 thin slices. Arrange 20 of these slices in the prepared baking pan or on the cookie sheet. Spoon some of the eggplant mixture onto each slice, then cover this layer of fish slices with the remaining slices. Tuck the edges of the slices under to make individual fish packages. Bake them for 2 minutes on each side.

Meanwhile, prepare the sauce. Separate the yolk and white of the hard-boiled egg. Squeeze the lemon juice into a bowl, add salt, pepper and the remaining olive oil. Add both types of fish eggs, half of the white and half of the yolk of the egg, the chives and the parsley, and combine.

Arrange 5 fish cocoons, like the petals of a flower, on each plate. In the center put 1 teaspoon of the tomato mixture. Spoon over the sauce. Crumble the remaining yolk and white of the egg and decorate. Garnish with the reserved cubed tomatoes.

LAVENDER ADDRESSES

[For information on the eight trails: Mme. Elizabeth Hauwuy, L'Association des Routes de la Lavande. Tel: (0) 475 26 65 90; FAX: (0) 475 26 32 67. B.P. 36, 26110 Nyons. E-mail: routes.lavande@educagre.fr.]

[Organically grown true lavender, distillation, apiculture: Lavande 1100, 84400 Lagarde d'Apt. Tel: (0) 490 75 01 42; FAX: (0) 490 75 01 42. Maurice Fra and family.]

[A fine historic garden: Prieuré de Salagon, 04300 Mane. Owned by the Conseil général. Tel: (0) 492 75 19 93; FAX: (0) 492 75 25 14. E-mail: salagon@karatel.fr.]

[Best food: La Bonne Etape, Chemin du Lac, 04160 Château Arnoux. Tel: (0) 492 64 00 09; FAX: (0) 492 64 37 37.]

[Dried flowers: Société Cassan La Combe du Pommier 04150, Simiane-la-Rotonde. Tel: (0) 492 75 91 70; FAX: (0) 492 75 92 23.]

ABOVE: *An oak tree stands among long lavender rows in the shimmering summer light.* FAR LEFT: *Alain Cassan near Simiane-la-Rotonde produces lovely bouquets of dried lavender.* LEFT: *Single-flowered hollyhocks will self-sow in any crack between two stones and spring up in every Provençal village.*

Lavender Trails

Lavender is a mountain crop—writer Jean Giono called it "the soul of the high country." Its story is multifaceted, involving traditions of folk medicine and perfumes, household uses, garden design and industry in the context of a constantly evolving rural economy. Today eight well-planned "lavender trails" draw all those interested in off-the-beaten-track discovery of country life in Provence, especially at cooler altitudes in summer heat. They offer picturesque landscapes and villages, distillation processes ranging from artisanal to ultra-scientific, aromatherapy centers, historic and botanic gardens, good cheap lodging and outstanding cuisine.

Until the twentieth century, lavender was simply picked wild on high slopes fertilized by the passage of grazing flocks. Today vast acres of long parallel lines seem like a distillation of the summer sky. But there is a whole range of lavender landscapes, from the small-scaled patchwork of little valleys near Sault to the vast industrial farms, juxtaposing deep purple lines with golden wheat, on the Plâteau de Valensole. Small mountain holdings specialize in "true" or species lavender (*Lavendula angustifolia* syn. *vera*). Some 300 small producers cultivate about 6,000 acres between five- and six-tenths of a mile high, covering almost 20 percent of the world market for true lavender essence, used largely by the perfume and pharmaceutical industries. True lavender is more subtle in its variations of fragrance and hue than the hybrid known as "lavandin," which thrives between one- and three-tenths of a mile high and is grown on about 33,000 acres producing some 1,200 tons of essence, representing 90 percent of the world's yearly crop. True lavender essence is soothing (for headaches, insect bites, etc.), whereas "lavandin" is tonic. Lavender still today has many faces, many lives—and many uses.

Lavender has many landscapes, from small mountain patchworks to the Plâteau de Valensole, where vast wheat fields alternate with plantations of the hybrid 'Super Blue.'

Food with the Famous in Arles II:
Frédéric Mistral and Alphonse Daudet

Frédéric Mistral, a contemporary of Van Gogh's, knew better than anyone "the local patois." Indeed, Mistral presided over the Félibrige movement to revive Provençal, the tongue of troubadours, as a Romance language in its own right. His efforts, begun in the 1860s, culminated in a Nobel Prize for Poetry in 1904.

Mistral and his companions cherished conviviality—that is to say, drinking, eating and the telling of tall tales. One outing in Arles involved several poets including Alphonse Daudet, whose *Letters From My Mill* (written in French) is still widely read today.

The young men reached Arles on foot at noon, famished and white with dust. They went straight to the Nord-Pinus restaurant where, Mistral recounts in his *Memoirs*, they were not too badly treated. The waiter annoyed them, however. Obviously worried about this Bohemian crew, "his head covered with pomade and two sideburns bristling like a whiskbroom," he hovered and hovered until Daudet, in a stentorian voice, demanded a silver platter "to put an ass on." The waiter disappeared.

The Nord-Pinus lunch was disappointing: "What is ridiculous in these hotels is that ever since traveling salesmen introduced northern tastes to the fixed menu, they now serve you the same dishes everywhere, whether in Avignon, in Angoulême, in Draguignan or in Brive-la-Gaillarde: carrot soup, veal with sorrel, half-cooked roast beef, cauliflower cooked in butter and other foods that have neither flavor nor savor. So if you want to find regional cooking again in Provence, our old cooking that's so tasty, you have to go to a cabaret where the common people eat."

That same evening, the poets went to a disreputable sailors' dive called the Comber's. The cook turned out to be "a slatternly woman and blind in one eye to boot." Mistral remarks: "For poets dreaming of beautiful Arlesiennes, this was somewhat disconcerting."

Worse yet, she claimed to have nothing at the ready.

"Nothing" turned out to be delicious, however: as appetizers, "two big Bellegarde onions, a plate of pickled peppers, some sharp cheese spread, pickled olives, fish roe from Martigues and several slices of braised cod." She would, she said, have made lamb blanquette, or an omelet, if she had been forewarned, but when people happen in on you "like hairs in a soup," they must take what they can get. And they did so with gusto. A pitcher of excellent wine from the Crau appeared. "In less than half an hour you could have lit a match on our cheeks."

Following was an eel stew, "salty as the sea and peppery as the devil, in which a shepherd's crook would have stood upright." The regular customers, who had fallen silent when these gentlemen arrived, finished their own meal of braised kid and began to sing tavern songs: "The girls of Avignon are just like melons: Of a hundred and fifty, there's not one that's ripe...."

Ironically, Mistral in later life came to be intimately and eternally linked with the Hôtel Nord-Pinus. In 1909, an imposing statue of the poet, looking for all the world like Buffalo Bill, was unveiled right in front of the hotel, as if he had just walked out the door. Mistral commented: "All that's missing is the suitcase." This statue still dominates the Place du Forum, though during the war the Germans removed it as a symbol of local resistance to occupying forces.

To be continued...see page 106.

Lizards in Life and Literature

As far as the eye could
see, the torrid white road
covered with its powdery
dust the gardens of olive
trees and little oaks, under
a round sun of burnished
silver that seemed to fill
up the sky. Not a speck
of shade, not a breath of
wind. Nothing but the
quivering of the hot air
and the strident cry of the
cicada's mad music, deafen-
ing, urgent, which seemed
to embody this immense,
vibrating radiance.
Alphonse Daudet,
LETTERS FROM MY MILL

In his novel about the wild shepherdess Manon of the Springs, Marcel Pagnol imagines the young girl taming a lizard—not one of the tiny, friendly creatures that dart in and out of dry stone walls, but the much more imposing *limbert* (sometimes called *lambert*). Manon sets out goat's milk on a tin plate and plays a few notes on her mouth organ. The lizard springs out from a distant bramble thicket, and "like a streak of light, ran towards the music and plunged its horny snout into the bluish milk of the gar-rigue." Ugolin, the peasant in love with Manon, watches this reenactment of beauty and the beast from behind a bush and wonders if she is a witch . . . or perhaps a fairy?

Lacerta lepida, characterized by its astonishing emerald green back and turquoise throat, is often more than two feet long and is the largest lizard in Europe. Living in the dry brushland of the garrigue, it seeks out underground springs and other spots of moisture. It feeds on big insects, smaller lizards, birds and mice, and is a ferocious hunter that never relinquishes its prey.

The limbert is not, however, averse to human company. Colette once saved such a dragon from her favorite cat and nursed it back to health. Colette and her lizard lunched to-gether daily; the animal developed a passion for fresh cream. But, at that point, afraid of ruining its health altogether, Colette took it back to the vineyard and stroked its head in farewell while the lizard's throat pulsed appreciatively. She then withdrew her hand, barely glimpsed a green comet, then found the spot suddenly, glaringly empty. She pictured the limbert carrying off the traces of her human solicitude, "which imagined itself disinterested. . . ."

The great green lizard of
Provence, with its turquoise
throat, becomes the friendly
companion and helper of many
Provençal gardeners.

A second spring, with a new season of growth through

 October, first frosts usually late November.

Fall sowing of wheat, oats, rye and barley.

Tree planting: "On Saint Catherine's Day

(November 25), all trees take root." The season when

Autumn in

Bacchus comes into his own again, for each year's grape

harvest. Fall colors in vineyards and orchards, each

variety of vine and fruit tree turning a different tone

of brilliant red, or rust, or gold. Wisps of wild clem-

atis over old walls. Quince paste and quince rolls, a

Provençal bread specialty. Jelly from the hips of wild

roses. Hanging fruit: catalpas, Judas trees, "snail trees"

(*Gleditsias*). Fields of fat, shiny cabbage

rows sheltered by cypresses, and in drier

soil, golden asparagus feathers mixed with vineyards

Provence is . . .

and orchards. Fruitwood still bright red and gold when

the leaves have gone. Colorful pyracantha hedges on

dull days, left arching or pruned into

flat bands, sometimes mixing yellow,

orange and red berries. The finest weather of the year.

Autumn

A bent wooden pitchfork leans casually against the stone wall
of the farmhouse at the Mas de Curebourg, an antique store at Isle-sur-la-Sorgue.

The Charterhouse of Bonpas: From Charlemagne to Côtes du Rhône

[Chartreuse de Bonpas, 84510 Caumont. Southeast of Avignon. Tel: (0) 490 23 09 59; FAX: (0) 490 23 19 97. Private property of Monsieur and Madame Casalis. Wine tasting is possible.]

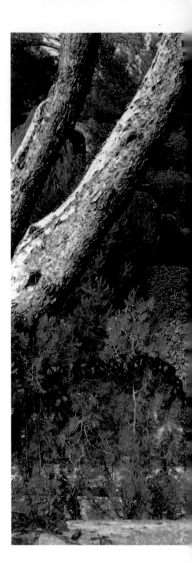

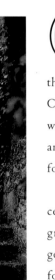

One of the most ancient roads in Europe, a drover's trail in Neolithic times, leads east from the Rhone valley toward the Alps. It crosses the mighty Durance River north of the market town of Cavaillon. For the Romans, this point on the Via Domitia was a ford of vital importance; they policed it well and guaranteed its safety. But once they left, it became a favorite spot for highway robbers.

In 751, nearby Avignon fell into the hands of the Saracens, invaders from North Africa, and subsequently, a great battle took place at just this spot. In 805, no less a general than Charlemagne collected the bones of the dead for burial, built a chapel and founded a monastery on the steep cliff overlooking the river, in order to shelter travelers and protect this ford. The brigands receded and traffic was successfully regulated. This stretch of the Durance, known until then as *maupas*, or "evil passage," now took the name of Bonpas.

The chapel and buildings have undergone many changes since they were first constructed. Monks of the Chartreuse order took over the premises in the fourteenth century, erecting the battlements that still remain. Although the monastery was partially destroyed during the Revolution, it was restored in the nineteenth century by ancestors of the

At the Charterhouse of Bonpas:
OPPOSITE, *steps leading to the
upper garden;* LEFT, *Virginia
creeper on the upper terrace by
the entrance to the yew parterre;*
LEFT BELOW, *the thick walls of
medieval battlements encircle the
domain; and* ABOVE, *a delicate
faun's head fountain in the
lower courtyard.*

After the feast of Saint Maurice (September 22), the
   days walk backward like a crayfish.
Le lendemain de la Saint-Maurice, le jour fait des
   pas d'écrivisses (marche à l'envers).
Lou lendeman de Sant-Maurice, lou jou fais
   pas d'escarabisso.

By Saint Michael's day (September 29), rain spoils the figs.
Pour la Saint-Michel, la pluie gâte les figues.
Pèr Sant Miquèu, li figo soun pèr li pichot aucèu.

present owners. Today, the property also includes an elegant terraced garden. Cut out of three steep levels, it comprises a large main courtyard, a formal parterre above, and a wild garden farther up. The chapel, rebuilt in the twelfth century, stands below the courtyard, on the outer edge of the ramparts.

The formal parterre, with its topiary cones, splendid statuary and sculpted basins, is the heart of the garden: It is laid out where monastic buildings once stood. The luminous, golden stone contrasts warmly with the somber greens of trimmed yew and box, and the soaring shapes of old, windbent stone pines. But this austere decor is enhanced by seasonal color: spring wisteria and redbuds bringing forth their mauve display against black wood; and the serpentine flames of virginia creeper in the fall. In addition, Monsieur and Madame Casalis are underplanting the severely pruned shapes with blue leadwort, Corsican rosemary, pink dianthus, and silvery bush convolvulus.

A modest sign points the way to this domain, north off the main Avignon–Apt road, just after the Avignon–Sud autoroute exit. Gracious stone pillars topped with urns mark the property. An avenue leads to a double-gated fortress entrance decorated with frescoes on its inner walls. In an office installed in an ancient guardhouse, information can be obtained about the owners' excellent Côtes du Rhône wines.

The Chartreuse de Bonpas dominates the surrounding landscape. It is visible from three sides, particularly from the autoroute at its foot. The ancient river ford it guards now serves modern traffic as well. And before long, the secret garden may be further invaded by the passage of the bullet train from Paris.

OPPOSITE: *Vineyards at Bonpas, with the fortress rising majestically beyond.* ABOVE: *The main courtyard entrance, near which wine tastings of the family vintages are held.*

The imposing Renaissance château of Suze-la-Rousse has now become a well-known university for the study of wines.

A University for Wine

[Université du Vin, Le Château, 26790 Suze-la-Rousse.
Tel: (0) 475 97 21 30; FAX: (0) 475 98 24 20.
E-mail: université.du.vin@wanadoo.fr.]

Scattered along the entire length of the narrow funnel of the Rhone valley is a series of châteaux. Some of these are picturesque strongholds dominating the road below, while others have been transformed throughout the centuries into elegant residences. In the past, the Château at Suze has been the site of heroic deeds and legends, but in 1978, thanks to the efforts of a farsighted group of professional vintners, agricultural researchers, businessmen and chambers of commerce, it became the Wine University of Suze-la-Rousse. They are responsible for the recent restoration of its distinguished medieval and Renaissance buildings.

The château is surrounded by a wonderfully wild oak wood and a garden displaying different types of vinestocks. Inside is one of the most beautiful and scientifically up-to-date tasting rooms, which, along with an equally modern laboratory and an extensive library, lies at the heart of the university's comprehensive training program. It is for professionals concerned with all phases of wine production, as well as for groups of amateurs who wish to perfect their knowledge of wine in general and of the Côtes du Rhône appellation in particular. Diploma programs include advanced technology, management and marketing, specialized law and training for sommeliers; also available are workshops of a half day to a week in regional wines, vinification, bottling, commercialization and distribution. Scientific efficiency has found a most romantic setting.

Saint Michael's day rains never stay in heaven.

Les pluies de la Saint-Michel ne restent jamais au ciel.

Li pluèio de Sant-Miquèu reston jamais au cèu.

Wine Festivals
of the Côtes du Rhône

Pierre Joseph Garidel, a doctor in Aix who published a treatise on botany in 1715, praised wine as "that liquor as precious as it is delicious, which offers us both medicinal nourishment and nourishing medicine, whose benefits affect the spirit as much as the body. . . ." The organizers and participants of Provence's many wine festivals would certainly agree. Most of the following *fêtes* incorporate a variety of other activities, such as parades in which the townspeople dress in local costumes.

Fall color and light in Provence create breathtaking compositions, with the taut lines of vineyards and orchards set against the scrubby evergreen hillsides called garrigue.

ABOVE: *Many people love Provençal landscapes best in the autumn, when fields are rich and ripe with the colors of harvest.*
RIGHT: *Grape harvesting in progress on the terraced slopes of northern Provence, in the Dentelles de Montmirail.*

MARCH	Vinsobres, local fête
APRIL	*April 20:* Villeneuve-lez-Avignon, Festival of Saint Marc
MAY	*May 1:* Bagnols-sur-Cèze, local fête
	Whitsun weekend (April or May): la Baume-de-Transit, competition of Tricastin wines
JUNE	*about June 15:* Saint-Victor-la-Coste, local fête
JULY	*first week:* Violès, local fête
	mid-July: Gordes (Côtes du Ventoux), Bourg-St-Andéol (local fête), Carpentras (Côtes du Ventoux), Buisson (local fête), Mondragon (local fête), Visan (local fête), Vacqueyras (festival for the local Côtes du Rhône appellation wines)
	late July: Pont-Saint-Esprit (local fête), Cairanne (local fête), Gordes (local fête), Caromb (festival for Côtes du Ventoux, in a different village each year)
AUGUST	*first half:* Valréas in combination with the lavender parade, Bédoin (local fête), Saint-Maurice-sur-Eygues (local fête), Ruoms (local fête), Mazan (local fête with a banquet), Vinsobres (festival of Côtes du Rhône–Villages appellations, in a different village each year)
	mid-month: Mirabel-aux-Baronnies, Séguret, Bédoin, Rasteau
SEPTEMBER	beginning, Visan (local fête)
NOVEMBER	*mid-month:* Wine and Food Fair at Vaison-la-Romaine
	late: Avignon Fête des Primeurs
	November 20: Sainte-Cécile-les-Vignes (wine and music festival), Tulette (Provençal mass)

For information, contact the Maison du Vin, 6, rue des Trois Faucons, 84024 Avignon. Tel: (0) 490 27 24 14; FAX: (0) 490 27 24 13. E-mail: promo@vivarhone.com. Web: www.vins-rhone.com.

The grapes are magnificent this year because of the fine autumn days. The vines I have just painted are green, purple and yellow, with violet bunches and branches of black and orange. On the horizon are some willows, the winepress a long, long way off, and the lilac silhouette of the distant town. In the vineyard there are little figures of women with red parasols, and other little figures of men working at the vintage with their cart.
Van Gogh, DEAR THEO

Food with the Famous in Arles III: From Picasso to M.F.K. Fisher

In the 1940s, the Hôtel Nord-Pinus was inherited by Jean Bessières, better known as Nello, the famous Médrano circus clown in Paris. He and his wife Germaine drew celebrities of every description: writers like Pagnol, film stars, singers such as Piaf, Brassens and Tino Rossi, sportsmen and royalty. Fernandel sat outside dipping anchovies into his pastis. King Farouk was reputed to have a *penchant* for Germaine. Picasso and Cocteau came for the bullfights, and the most famous toreadors greeted the crowds from the balcony of room number 10, always reserved for them. The hotel bar "Le Cintra" still has souvenirs of this time. Cocteau called the Nord-Pinus "a hotel with a soul." No one mentions the food.

Nello died in 1969. Soon after, two famous food critics who knew nothing of the hotel's history tried it and found it wanting. One was French, one American.

In the fall of 1970, influential food critic Robert Courtine came to Arles to cover the annual rice festival for the Parisian newspaper *Le Monde*. Courtine admired "the pretty Arlesian girls" but judged the food at the Nord-Pinus "as mediocre as it is in 99.99 percent of French hotels." Unaware that he was following in Mistral's footsteps, Courtine went off in search of advice. Dropping the names of some Pigalle chums to the Corsican owner of a low-life bar, he arranged a Provençal feast for the next day "in some sort of suburban dive"—perhaps at Trinquetaille?

Lunch had been ordered for six. Courtine arrived with four colleagues to find a meal prepared for twelve. It was a Grand

Autumn sunlight is soft and warm on old walls of hilltowns and villages.

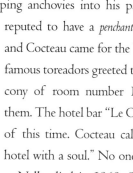

For Saint Martin's day
(November 11), chest-
nuts and new wine.

Pour la Saint-Martin,
la chataigne et le
vin nouveau.

A sant Martin, la castagne
et liu nouvèu vin.

For Saint Catherine s day
(November 25), the oil
is in the olive.

Pour la Sainte-Catherine,
l'huile est dans l'olive.

Pèr Santo-Caterino, l'oli
es dins l'oulivo.

Aioli: Besides the cod, there were snails, small blanched squid, hard-boiled eggs, quantities of boiled carrots, potatoes, sunchokes, string beans, beets, chick peas, artichokes, cauliflower and boiled leg of lamb with mountains of garlic mayonnaise. Locals had assembled to sneer at the Parisian journalists. But, Courtine claims, the city folk ate everything in sight—added by a *trou du milieu* of strong local *marc*. They were applauded.

For his newspaper column, Courtine wrote up the minister of agriculture's speech as if he had actually heard it, only discovering on his return to Paris that the minister had canceled his trip altogether. No one noticed.

Also in 1970 but at Christmas, American food writer M. F. K. Fisher came to the Hôtel Nord-Pinus. Then, almost everything was closed for Christmas—including the hotel's restaurant. She liked her room, which had been Jean Cocteau's, but complained of a desk clerk who never looked her in the eye. Like Henry James before her, she wished she had stayed at the Hotel du Forum next door. There she enjoyed the sausage of Arles with radishes, butter, and olives, good braised endive, and one of the best apple tarts of her life, accompanied by a half bottle of Tavel.

She too asked advice of market people on where to get local food but found the Arlesian women tough and hard. The sadness of her stay was in part her own, she admitted, but was also destined to mark the next decades of life at the Hôtel Nord-Pinus. New beginnings for the hotel and its cuisine were in store, thanks to the timely intervention of…a beautiful Arlesian woman. *To be continued...see page 152.*

The inner courtyard of Rochegude castle is full of niches, basins and fountains, set off by sculpture and simple local plants: santolinas and Virginia creepers.

ABOVE: *The luminous yellow autumn foliage of the mulberry tree. Its leaves were traditionally gathered in spring by farm women to feed to silk worms.* RIGHT: *Migrating flocks of sheep are still a common sight throughout the Midi.*

Transhumance:
Age-Old Migration of Sheep

Transhumance is the name given to the seasonal migration of sheep over long distances: up to mountain pastures in summer, down into valleys in winter. The trails followed were established in the dawn of history. Some historians believe that it was the mountain dwellers who first started the practice of moving their charges to the lowlands for the winter. Others suggest that the animals themselves may have naturally begun the practice in search of food.

In Provence, by the mid-nineteenth century, as many as 400,000 animals would travel along the various routes, or *draios*. Such numbers could not migrate twice yearly without inflicting some damage: in fact, records of litigation between shepherds and farmers exist dating back to the Middle Ages. Certainly the herds' overuse of pasturelands led to vegetal impoverishment and loss of topsoil. Since sheep and goats eat almost everything in sight, except for some prickly, strong-tasting plants, their migration, unfortunately, has played a major role in creating the barren *garrigue* of today.

Transhumance constituted an important part of traditional rural life. French historian Fernand Braudel describes it as "the typical opening onto the outside world of primitive communities." Over the years, specific customs, costumes, even festivals became associated with this age-old practice. And until the early part of this century, the passage of the animals was an extraordinary spectacle to behold. The sheep were classed by sex, age and variety, with the weakest leading the way. Each category was further subdi-

vided into groups of 1,600 to 2,400 head, with one shepherd and one dog assigned to watch over 400 animals. The dogs were enormous and supposedly tough enough to fight a wolf. Long-haired donkeys wearing bells carried the supplies. The rams, too, were bedecked with headdresses, and the sheep were marked with different colors of ocher to show ownership. Alphonse Daudet has left one of the most vivid descriptions of the returning flocks in his *Letters from My Mill.* He observes them coming along the ancient Roman Aurelian Way, through Eyguières, then Le Paradou. "The road itself seemed on the march . . . the old rams first, leading with their horns, with a wild look to them; behind came the bulk of the sheep, the mothers somewhat weary with their suckling lambs underfoot; the mules, with red pompons, carried the newborn in baskets on their backs that rocked like cradles by the slow rhythm of the march; then the dogs, all in a sweat, their tongues hanging to the ground, and two shepherds, great rogues draped in homespun russet coats that reached to their feet like great capes."

Even in Daudet's time, transhumance met with opposition from agronomists, who feared for the forest land of the Alps, or who were interested in selecting varieties of sheep for qualities other than their road hardiness. The defenders of transhumance, however, insisted that the sheep remained healthier if they migrated, and objected to the cost of fodder in areas where summer drought was inevitable. Today, of course, the automobile has provided both the obstacle and

BELOW: *Vineyards on the north slopes of the Luberon hills look toward the Mont Ventoux. The Calavon river valley possesses a particularly rich rural patchwork, spread out at the foot of its fashionable hilltowns.*
OPPOSITE: *Traveling to and from mountain pastures during transhumance, the famous biennial migration, sheep are marked for identification with ocher and colorful pompoms.*

Meal shared by a land-
owner and his shepherd in
a stone shelter, when the
flocks come down from the
mountains in November:

Arnaviel offered me a
ripe ewe's cheese wrapped
in fresh leaves. We lit a
fire between two stones.
I had some late September
figs, already a bit dry,
but sweet, rich with honey.
The bread was hard but
smelled of the wheat. The
spring water was light on
the tongue, with its sweet,
pure taste of the rock.

As the weather was
very clear, the air stayed
calm and the smoke of
our fire rose straight up
through the chimney of
our stone shelter.

Henri Bosco,
LE MAS THEOTIME

the solution to the practice: transhumance, insofar as it persists, is generally done by truck.

Flocks of sheep can still be seen throughout the Midi,
even near villages transformed by the wealthy, the artistic,
and the cosmopolitan. The average motorist has every
chance of encountering the animals on small country roads

in the Alpilles or the Luberon. One friendly shepherd
guards his charges on the high pastures overlooking the
dramatic village of Saignon, near a road that might seem
remote, but along which toot cars with surprising regular-
ity. Almost every driver knows him, and stops to chat,
whether antiques dealer, painter or café owner. It seems as
if the shepherd, living on the outskirts of a highly sophisticated and touristic community, has discovered his own
outdoor café.

Botanical Trails
in Historic Mountains

[Notre-Dame-de-Groseau: a mountain lake off the road between Carpentras and Vaison-la-Romaine, leading northeast toward the white cone of Mont Ventoux. Just over one mile outside Malaucène on the D974.]

Backed by the southwest flanks of Mont Ventoux, about 1,300 feet high, lies a famous spring, a deep turquoise pool that spreads its cool waters amidst rocky outcrops. This spot was much appreciated by the Romans as a summer resort, and became the site of a monastery in the seventh century. Clement v, the first pope to settle in Avignon, built his summer residence here in the early fourteenth century, around an older chapel. Fragments of these structures, with elegant sculptural detailing, still stand by the approach road. Even more strikingly poised on the steep slope above is an immaculate, ruined plaster works, erected in 1919 and abandoned in 1950, presiding over a gypsum quarry that had already been exploited in Roman times.

In high summer, Notre-Dame-de-Groseau is crowded with swimmers and families picnicking on stone slab tables under the spreading canopies of old plane trees. Off season, it has a peaceful mood. The addition of two botanical trails leading through the nearby hills, one of which takes about half an hour to walk, the other taking more than an hour, has added to its appeal. Even the shorter one reveals a wealth of plants: wild clematis, junipers, viburnums, the brilliant blue stars of aphyllanthes in May, wild aromatics, brooms, three kinds of oaks, as well as two different pines, and much more. Orientation tables explain the evolution

In September, if the water-willow flowers, the grapes ripen well and the peasant is all smiles.

En septembre, si l'osier fleurit, le raisin mûrit et le paysan rit.

En setèmbre, se lou vege flouris, lou rain s'amaduro et lou paisan ris.

OPPOSITE AND RIGHT: *The mountain spring at Notre Dame de Groseau near Malaucène, where first Romans, then a fourteenth-century Pope, once bathed, remains a popular watering place today.*

of the local vegetation, and reforestation plans that include fire prevention in the area. Recently 800 wild cherry (*Prunus avium*) and 500 false acacia (*Robinia pseudoacacia*) have been planted. In some places, experiments with new cypress varieties are being supervised by the agricultural services in Antibes.

The geology of the site is equally impressive. The gypsum dates from at least 27,000,000 years ago, while the stone fragments may be Roman or Renaissance . . . or possibly modern cement imitation. The pool itself has a rough, grottolike setting, with natural stone eruptions creating cool reflections in the multitoned water.

The old plaster works and their wild surroundings (an area of about 55 acres) have been purchased by the General Council of the Vaucluse. Plans are afoot to make it a center for nature study: it is already a stopping point for hikers and horseback riders.

A simple restaurant across the road from the spring serves a Ventoux salad, composed of mountain ham and cheese, curly, crisp escarole and local olive oil. The autumn air is fresh and sweetly scented. Sometimes a dog may be heard barking in the distance, or a donkey hee-hawing, but otherwise all is tranquil. This is a place—in the off-season—for enjoyment of all the senses.

Splendidly patterned vineyards with poplar and cypress hedging spread out against the rocky hillside beyond. In view of such glorious fall landscapes, many people consider autumn the most beautiful season in Provence.

Art at Home:
The Gallery Lestranger

*[Galerie Lestranger et Comptoir de Lestranger, Place Jean de Renaud,
13210 Saint-Rémy-de-Provence. Tel: (0) 490 92 57 14;
FAX: (0) 490 92 69 17. Owner: Catherine Binda-Sterling. E-mail:
cst@lestranger.fr. Web: www.lestranger.fr. By appointment only.]*

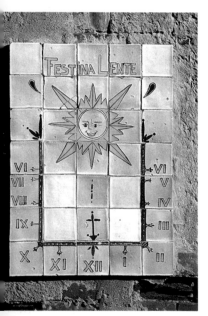

This cheerful sundial decorates the ocher-washed wall of the Vernin tile factory, west of Apt.

Wisteria encircles Catherine Binda-Sterling's courtyard fountain outside her gallery in Saint-Rémy-de-Provence.

Imagine an apple orchard somewhere in southwestern France where the Louvre's greatest masterpieces stand propped against tree trunks. This was Catherine Binda-Sterling's earliest experience of the French countryside. Her father, Charles Sterling, was curator at the Louvre. In 1941, during the German occupation of France, the museum's collections were spirited off to a country château. But the oil paintings needed regular airing...when not stored in crates under the canopied bed where little Catherine slept. When the family fled to New York, where Catherine's father became curator of the French collections at the Metropolitan Museum of Art, she herself trained as a ballerina —so successfully that she danced with Balanchine's New York City Ballet. Later in postwar Paris, Brussels and Rome, she switched to art and became one of France's most valued restorers.

Catherine kept dreaming of masterpieces among apple trees. In 1991, she opened her gallery in Saint-Rémy-de-Provence to create her own version of *l'art aux champs*, or art in the country. Catherine feels at home in Provence where Roman ruins may stand among olive trees and vines as they often do in the eighteenth- and nineteenth-century paintings she displays in her spacious house. The high standards of her collections are evident in her inclusion at such prestigious art shows as the Salon des Beaux Arts, where she is the only gallery owner not based in Paris, London, or New York.

A Poet in Provence

I wander aimlessly from
lane to lane
Bending a careful ear to
ancient times
The same cicadas sang in
Caesar's reign
Upon the walls the same
sun clings and climbs...

What bliss it is in this
world of song
To brush against the chalk
of walls
What bliss to be a human
poet lost among
Cicadas trilling with a
Latin lisp.

—Vladimir Nabokov, 1923

Evident also in the exhibitions she has arranged in Saint-Rémy are the beautiful catalogues published in conjunction with these.

There is much more to the Lestranger Gallery than the tourist image of "quilts and lavender," but Catherine does sell fine quilts as well as antique tableware in her gallery. Everyone in her family loves to cook. Above all, she takes pleasure in a way of life in which everyday objects, great art, good food and the soft murmur of her garden fountain are all one. She would not have bought the house without the garden. She loves not only to work in it but also to contemplate it from the second-floor balcony, where it beckons to her from a well of fragrant sunshine.

The gallery is named for Pierre-Cyprien Lestranger, a nineteenth-century humanist and art collector who may have lived there. For Catherine Binda-Sterling, with her strong sense of communion with objects, places and plants, he still does. The Lestranger Gallery today offers all the calm beauty of a Chardin still life translated into Provençal.

Catherine Binda-Sterling's art gallery is also her home, with windows opening right onto the garden below.

The Olive Harvest

For millennia, farmers all over the Mediterranean have been picking olives—green ones in October, brown ones in November, black and oily ones in December. Mentioned in both the Bible and the *Odyssey*, olives were dedicated to Athena by the Greeks (who used the oil in wrestling matches), and to Minerva by the Romans. Hercules fought his monsters—in southern Provence among other places—with a club of olive wood. And while the wild variety of the tree (*Olea europea oleaster*) grew naturally in Provence, it produced spiny, sour fruit with little oil. Not until the Greeks arrived around 600 B.C. did the native population learn the art of grafting.

Today, an olive tree that has been grafted and cultivated and is in full production can yield 65 pounds of olives a year (giving roughly six quarts of oil). Although olive trees can survive almost anywhere, and are nearly indestructible except when hit by hard, late frosts, those grown for fruit or oil need a lot of attention. A Provençal proverb imagines the olive tree saying to the farmer: "Feed my feet and I'll wet your whistle!" Sheep manure works wonders, as does good pruning. It is said that the silvery branches of the olive tree must be kept open enough so that a swallow can fly through without touching its wings. With such loving care, an olive tree can be expected to enter into full production at the age of . . . 35 years.

Olive culture is declining in France, like so many other old customs: Of the 16,000,000 trees thought to be growing there in the early part of the century, only 5,000,000 remain. But the commune of Mouriès alone, in the southern Alpilles, has more than 80,000 olive-producing trees, a

ABOVE: *Olives that are allowed to ripen on the tree turn black and wizened, thick with the oil that pressing at the local mill will soon extract. Cold pressing produces the finest oil.* OPPOSITE: *The olive harvest marks the year's end. Still often carried out by hand today, it requires considerable attention and skill.*

The olive harvest—an epic event. From the steel gray branch to the clay jar, the olive pours through a hundred hands, rushing on in torrents, piling up the weight of its black waters in attics where old beams complain in the night. On the edge of this great river of ripe fruit that streams through the villages, all our people sing together.
Jean Giono, POEM OF THE OLIVE

world record. Most Provençal chefs, however, prefer to get their oil in Maussane, or Fontvieille, towns located in the Alpilles between Avignon and Arles.

Generations ago, trees reached as high as 50 feet, but new varieties and present-day pruning practices restrict their growth to about 15 feet. As a result, harvesting olives is much easier today. The old practice of using long rods to beat high branches proved detrimental to the trees, which produce only on new, soft wood. But even now, in many areas, some harvesters of ripe olives climb into the trees to shake the branches while others (usually the women) collect the fruit that falls on nets spread directly on the ground below. To harvest the crop mechanically, with shakers, vibrators and aspirators, the orchards must be specially planted and spaced from the start.

Green olives must be picked off the trees by hand, as they will not readily shake down and will bruise easily. A skilled harvester can collect up to 30 pounds an hour from heavily laden trees bearing a variety that detaches easily. Labor costs obviously count high in the production of oil.

Traditionally, olive picking is a family activity, sometimes extending to neighbors from the same village. Naturally enough, there is time for festivity—usually in the form of that favorite banquet food in Provence: a massive *aïoli.*

Olives are picked first green, then brown, then black as they ripen on the tree. They are then cured to remove bitterness and blended with various herbs and condiments. The resulting variety can be found in any country market, as here at Saint-Rémy-de-Provence.

Curing Olives at Home

RIGHT: *High avenues of plane trees embellish every Provençal château and manor house, as here at Roussan, a hotel near Saint-Rémy. Their leaves are the bane of many gardeners—large, tough, plentiful, and impossible to compost.*

OPPOSITE TOP: *Autumn colors in Provence draw not only on foliage but on many types of red berries and the solid presence of evergreens. Here they enhance the mellow shutters of a house near Saint-Rémy.*

Olives change in color from green to brown to black on the tree as they ripen, but at no time during this process are they edible, because of their bitterness. To dispel this unpleasant taste, they are "cured," usually with potassium obtained from wood ashes (either from vine or olive wood, never cypress). Traditionally, an equal amount of olives and ashes were mixed in a bowl with enough water to make a paste, which was then stirred several times a day for two days. When the flesh of the fruit came off easily under pressure from a nail, the olives were carefully washed and soaked in clear water that was changed twice daily, for another week. At

the end of that time, the fruit were ready for their final salt bath: Two pounds of sea salt were added to ten quarts of water, then the mixture was boiled for 15 minutes along with fennel, orange peel, coriander, bay leaf or sage . . . whatever fancy preferred. The olives were added once the mixture cooled and then were put into storage for at least a week. Removed with the characteristic perforated dipping spoon (made with olive wood, of course) so as not to disturb the brew, they could be expected to last until Easter.

As the days passed, the bloodied wound of the maple spread, the roads were edged with two streaks of blood. A secret inflammation swelled up within the earth. The poplars were lit with a cold flame, more sparkling than that of the sun. Orange embers snaked among the hedges. The wounded fields turned blue along the streams. A heavy dust of autumn crocuses stifled the fields under its yellow vapor. The forest remained, it remained with its thick, solid pines. We envied the men of the forest, for our weak trees in the

The "Bistrot à Michel"

[Bistrot à Michel, Grand Rue, 84220 Cabrières d'Avignon. Tel: (0) 490 76 82 08. Owner: Michel Bosc. Chef: Ian Bosc.]

Discovered by artists even before World War II, the hilltown of Gordes has become one of the most chic vacation spots in the world. How does rural life survive in this rarefied atmosphere? This restaurant provides one answer: Here celebrities and millionaires rub shoulders with antiques dealers, tourists . . . and local farmers, all providing part of the show for each other. Famous chef Georges Blanc lunched at the bistrot when visiting the local truffle markets. Writer Peter Mayle made this café the focus for his essay on *pastis,* the local anise-flavored drink. To the right as you go in, owner Michel Bosc stands at the bar, discussing seasonal topics, such as hunting or truffle digging with villagers, while his wife presides at the cash register opposite.

Monsieur Bosc apprenticed as a chef at several famous establishments before deciding to return to his native village to open his own place. Now his son Ian, equally well-trained, produces succulent and original dishes, served by his sister to cosmopolitan customers at ten marble-topped tables. The bistrot style has been carefully maintained: The walls are packed with framed movie posters featuring Pagnol and Raimu, cartoons about life in the Luberon, original oils wih bullfight themes and a poster from the Museum of Modern Art in New York. In the center stands the classic buffet, laden with assorted bottles of aperitifs, brandies and liqueurs. Each table has a colorful bouquet: squash and mountain flowers for autumn. The wine list is handwritten and a bit smudged. The *patron* may come by as

meadows, our copses, the poplars of our fountains, all that was now aflame. And with each passing day, the burning trees grew less rust-colored, more yellow, slighter. . . . One could feel that all that was about to be extinguished.
Jean Giono,
RONDEUR DES JOURS

Poplar pillars grow as windbreak hedges along many country roads in Provence, making a delicate fretwork against a mistral-blue sky.

you dine, reverently carrying a huge sausage to show the men at the bar.

The Bosc cuisine presents the same mix of sophistication and country origins as does its decor. In the fall, stuffed pheasant may be offered, with onion marmalade, vanilla-flavored quince and potato pancakes. Or, the menu may feature an entrée of wild duck neck stuffed with chickpeas, served with pigs' feet cracklings and mixed greens. The main dish might be lamb petals, with garlic prepared in three different ways (as custard, as fritters and simply fried), followed by a small filler of quince paste covered with lukewarm chocolate. A Côte du Lubéron Val Joanis wine would nicely complement the meal, which might conclude with this light but flavorful fruit dessert.

Village fountains, many beautifully carved, often stand near communal washing basins at town entrances as here, at Mallemort du Comtat.

APPLE BUTTER WITH THYME AND SAFFRON

▲▲▲▲▲▲▲▲

Serves 6

2½ *pounds Jonathan, winesap, or other flavorful apples*
Juice of 1 lemon
1¼ *pounds sugar*
1 *teaspoon thyme flowers or leaves*
⅓ *teaspoon saffron*

Peel and dice the apples. Put them in a glass or pottery bowl and sprinkle with lemon juice. Add the sugar and mix with a wooden spoon. Pour the apple mixture into a thick-bottomed pan and simmer, covered, for 45 minutes, checking regularly, until a syrup forms. Remove the cover and continue simmering for an additional hour, stirring frequently, until the "butter" thickens. Remove the mixture from the heat and add the thyme and saffron. Cover the pan again and let the mixture cool. Serve cold.

*Evergreens, trees and shrubs—
often cypresses, box and
laurustinus—protect farm-
houses from winter winds and
anchor them to the landscape.*

SCOURTINS: An Unusual Craft

[La Scourtinerie, 36, la Maladrerie, 26110 Nyons. Tel: (0) 475
26 33 52; FAX: (0) 475 26 20 72. Owner: Monsieur J. Fert.
Visits by appointment.]

For many people, the northern boundary of Provence is determined by the range of the olive tree's successful growth, and the town of Nyons lies close to this edge. Because of the configuration of surrounding mountains and narrow valleys, Nyons enjoys a favorable microclimate that permits even palm trees to survive. Its extensive olive orchards have produced oil that has been praised for centuries; indeed, it is the only area to have a controlled appellation for this product.

As part of the process of pressing, the numerous local mills long used a filtering system of woven, flattened baskets, called *scourtins*. One family factory still makes them. Situated in an elegant seventeenth-century domain, shaded by majestic plane trees, its vast workshop is full of revolving metal drums with spokes. This largely nineteenth-century machinery produces mats, like flattened berets, that are about 15 inches wide, densely woven and prickly.

The first scourtins were of straw, fabric or alfalfa fiber. But with the advent of the Industrial Revolution, wooden equipment was replaced with steel in the mills, and more resistant material was called for. In 1882, Ferdinand Fert, a weaver and locksmith in Nyons, devised the modern scourtin, using sisal, or coconut fiber. He also invented the machinery to manufacture it, and founded the family business that still operates on the same site today.

Hidden in a remote part of an out-of-the-way town, this activity might seem purely local. But, typically, in Provence, which has always allied mountain and sea, the production

I have done another canvas, AN AUTUMN GARDEN, with two cypresses, bottle-green, shaped like bottles, and three little chestnut trees, a little yew with pale lemon foliage, two bushes blood red with scarlet-purple leaves; some sand, some grass, and some blue sky. . . . The falling of leaves is beginning; you can see the trees turning yellow, and the yellow increasing every day. It is at least as beautiful as the orchards in bloom.

Van Gogh, DEAR THEO

Old Provençal farmhouses, like this one at the foot of the Luberon, expanded piece by piece over centuries, sometimes turning into entire hamlets.

of these sisal mats depends on Mediterranean commerce: The raw materials come from the Malabar coast of India. For it is there that the best quality of coconut fiber can be found. During the monsoon period, which lasts several months, it undergoes a long soaking process, ending with pure rainwater. The final result is sisal that resists rot, takes dyes better and does not rust the machinery.

By the mid-1950s, there were several scourtin factories still operating in the south, and the Fert family decided to invest in improved equipment. Then came the terrible frosts of 1956, which destroyed so many ancient olive orchards in Provence. In addition, almost an entire year's production of scourtins already shipped to North Africa was lost at the outbreak of the Algerian War. Monsieur Fert, son of the founder, decided not to despair; instead, he diversified, concentrating on the fabrication of doormats and rugs, tinting them in a wide range of bright colors. He also began to import Indian crafts, which he sells alongside Provençal products in the family shop. In the 1970s, when drought in India threatened to cut off his supply of sisal, Monsieur Fert bypassed his British middleman and went to see his supplier for himself. The result was a surprising tale of country cunning on an international scale, which might well have happened a hundred years ago.

Arriving in India, Monsieur Fert discovered a convent where young women from remote country villages were

The famous Mas du Juge, the farmstead where Nobel prize-winning poet Frédéric Mistral spent an idyllic childhood, described in his memoirs.

Southwest wind, dry one minute, wet the next.
Vent du sud-ouest, sec une minute, le bain après.
Labechado une seco, uno bagnado.

sent for three years of schooling by parents who could not afford to give them dowries. The nuns, in conjunction with the Institut Catholique, willingly trained their charges in the production of sisal as part of their education, thus providing the Fert factory with its raw materials and the women with savings toward their dowries, as well as equipment and a craft that they could pursue in later life. The school has since expanded from 8 to 600 pupils.

Monsieur Fert relishes these international exchanges between country villages on different continents, and the continuity of an ancient local tradition. In his office, a stained glass panel depicts olive pressing using scourtins; it was copied from a Roman mosaic. The founding ancestor viewed his craft as a harmony between man, the tree and the earth, and his descendants still feel this very strongly.

The premises of the factory are vast: They occupy three levels. A showroom has been installed on the first floor, where the temperature remains constant in all seasons, and a lively videotape explains the history of the business and the evolution of its techniques. At one end can be seen remnants of an old mill wheel, and outdoors, a neglected formal garden from the days when the house was a noble residence. Today, with the new techniques employing centripetal pressure, the need for scourtins is disappearing in olive oil mills. But Monsieur Fert has plans for the future. He proudly shows drums of sisal netting that he has just imported: These can be used by gardeners for planting on difficult slopes, or for delicate sowings during dry spells to encourage germination. Discovery and innovation are themselves this family's richest heritage. The owner's daughter is now in charge of most of the current production.

But in my native Provence, pinewoods and olive groves turn yellow only when they die, and the first rains of September, which wash anew the green branches, bring back the month of April. On the barren hillsides, the thyme, rosemary, juniper and kermes oak keep their green foliage forever, while the wild lavender stays everblue. It is in the depths of the silent valleys that furtive autumn sneaks in; he takes advantage of rain at night to turn the little vineyard yellow, or the four peach trees, which then look sick, and in order to hide his arrival all the better he brings a blush to the naive arbutus, which begins to flower anew even as its berries turn red.

Marcel Pagnol,
MY MOTHER'S CASTLE

ZUCCHINI AND FENNEL SOUP

▲▲▲▲▲▲▲

Serves 4

4 small or 2 medium zucchini
1 fennel bulb, with a few leaves
1 leek
1 tablespoon butter
4 cups good chicken broth
1 teaspoon cornstarch
1 egg yolk
½ cup heavy cream

Wash, trim and cut the zucchini into thin rounds. Remove the outer leaves of the fennel and leek. Wash the vegetables carefully and chop them finely; include a small green section of the leek. Reserve the fennel leaves.

Melt the butter in a thick-bottomed pan, add the vegetables, and cook them gently, without browning (add 1 tablespoon of water, if necessary), for 15 to 20 minutes.

Set aside some zucchini rounds for decoration. Put the remainder of the vegetables through a food mill or food processor. Return them to the pan with the chicken broth. Bring the mixture gently to a boil and simmer for 5 minutes.

Cairanne Vintners' Cooperative

[Cave des Coteaux, 84200 Cairanne. Tel: (0) 490 30 82 05; FAX: (0) 490 30 74 03.]

The hilltown of Cairanne stands silhouetted against the dramatic shapes of Mont Ventoux and the Dentelles de Montmirail, dominating vast stretches of surrounding vineyards. Highest of the Rhone wine villages, with about 800 inhabitants today, it is known to have existed in 739, when it was called Queroana. Its wine cooperative, started in 1929, counts among the most active and appreciated of the region. Some 300 vintners sell three-quarters of their wine to the French market, and export the rest (much is sold by correspondence, in lovely gift packages). Three categories are produced: "vin de pays," labeled Principauté d'Orange; Côtes du Rhône; and the Côtes du Rhône–Villages wines, labeled Cairanne. The reds are the best known, with their ruby or dark carmine color, and their characteristic echo of strawberry and raspberry flavors. They are a blend of Grenache, Cinsault, Syrah, Mourvèdre and Carignan grapes, while Clairette, white Grenache and Bourboulenc are used for the whites. Also produced here are floral and peppery rosés, and a natural sweet aperitif wine called Cairador. The modern cave situated in the lower village displays many medals won by its wines all over Europe. The prestigious gastronomic guide *Gault et Millau* regularly commends it.

In a small bowl, beat together the cornstarch, the egg yolk and the cream in that order. Add a small amount of hot soup to the egg-yolk mixture, stirring constantly. Then pour the egg-yolk mixture into the soup and keep stirring until it thickens. Pour the soup into four bowls and garnish each with some zucchini rounds and fennel leaves.

The village of Cairanne stands dramatically silhouetted against the cloud-topped Mont Ventoux, above its colorful vineyards. Its vintners' co-operative is much appreciated for Côtes du Rhône wines.

Vineyards like script on the slopes, or the designs of

Persian carpets, always variation within formal patterns.

Lunch on the patio in warm sunshine, followed by snow

the next day. Persimmon trees with multicolored foli-

age; once the leaves have fallen, brilliant orange

Winterin

globes, like Christmas tree ornaments, against black

wood and a deep blue sky. Bell ring-

ing on February 5 in Mistral's village,

Maillane, so that Saint Agatha will ward off storms.

New Year's Day, when traditionally a stewed rooster is

served, accompanied by twelve partridges, thirty truf-

fles ("blacker than the soul of the damned") and thirty

 fried eggs . . . to represent months, nights

and days. Fragrant, fluffy, tiny yellow balls

of mimosa, like a promise of summer sun, dotting the

Provence is . . .

landscape, followed by the almond blossoms of late

February. The killing of the family pig, traditionally

part of the "fat" side of Carnival, which

ends with Mardi Gras. The mistral, the

mistral and again the mistral. . . .

Winter

*An elegant portal at the Château de la Nerthe at Châteauneuf-du-Pape
separates the stately manor house and park from the wintry vineyards that surround it on all sides.*

The Magnificent Saint Andrew Abbey Garden of Villeneuve

[Abbaye de Saint-André, 30400 Villeneuve-lez-Avignon.
Tel: (0) 490 25 55 95. Open 10 A.M. to 12 P.M. and 2 P.M. to 5 P.M.
October thru March, in summer until 6 P.M. Closed Mondays.
Private property of Mademoiselle Roseline Bacou.]

Opposite the city of Avignon, overlooking the Rhone, an impressive white limestone crenellated wall crowns the hilltop at Villeneuve. These fourteenth-century ramparts protect the much older village of Saint Andrew, which originally sprang up around the dwelling of a sixth-century hermit, Sainte Césarie. Today, only a picturesque ghost town remains within the walls, along with the abbey originally founded around the saint's shrine. Unexpected behind its forbidding gate, this magnificent property with its terraced gardens is open to the public, and has become a favorite place for local people to have their wedding pictures taken.

The imposing buildings were formerly part of the twelfth- to seventeenth-century premises of a Benedictine community. But they are just a vestige of the original domain, which was dismantled at the time of the French Revolution—indeed, around 1910, much of modern Villeneuve was built with stones from the abbey, which was then used as a convenient quarry. A succession of post-Revolutionary owners made the most varied uses of this site: One man built an observatory in an attempt to see the island of Elba. An impoverished religious community lived here without

Winter is no bastard, if it doesn't come sooner, it comes later.

L'hiver n'est pas bâtard, s'il ne vient pas de bonne heure, il vient plus tard.

L'ivèr es pas bastard, se noun vèn d'ouro, vèn plus tard.

OPPOSITE: *A Romanesque chapel at the summit of the steep Saint Andrew Abbey garden in Villeneuve-lez-Avignon.*

ABOVE: *The stone pergola of the Abbey garden, underplanted with iris.*

LEFT: *Spring in the Saint André gardens bursts forth with purple-pink Judas trees outlined against the fortress walls.*

water, sustained by wild herbs and dandelions. And then, in the early twentieth century, an art collector began its restoration. His friend Emile Bernard (companion also of Van Gogh and, especially, Cézanne) decorated the interior with a set of frescoes. Another friend, poet Paul Claudel, stayed at the abbey when visiting his poor sister, the misunderstood sculptress, who was condemned to the asylum in Avignon. By 1916, two talented women, a poet and a painter, had begun redesigning the gardens.

Their main achievement was the rose parterre, which has recently received an award for period gardens. Fan-shaped, it extends between elegant rococo stone basins, and is best seen from the terrace above, where the main buildings once stood. This acknowledgment of an architectural axis long since disappeared lends magic to a garden that is full of echoes and ghosts. The present owner, Mademoiselle Bacou, a distinguished art-historian, had the courage to dig into the hillside to uncover two ruined chapels with the sanctuary of Sainte Césarie. Banked by fragrant yellow coronilla in March, and encircled with cypresses, these are the most important ruins but not the only ones. A series of steps and paths leads uphill, past iris-lined olive orchards (some trees are more than 400 years old) to a twelfth-century chapel at the top.

This fine old Provençal garden is an ideal place to discover local styles and vegetation. Intimate yet elegant, enclosed and protected from the wind but with marvelous views of the Rhone valley south and east, it is always varied, never fussy. The subtle, luminous grays of the stone itself set the tone, for which dark vegetation provides the foil. The garden's lines, levels and perspectives are emphasized by the different greens of its olive trees, cypresses,

The sanctuary of Sainte Césarie, a ruined chapel with remnants of tombs, is a dramatic feature of the garden's middle levels. It is backed by the fourteenth-century ramparts which still encircle the old town.

laurustines and box, highlighted with color in all seasons: Redbuds overhang the rococo basins, cascades of white banksia roses cover a stone-pillared arbor, and white doves often circle above. Wisteria, lavenders, oleanders, centranthus all play their part as each season unfolds. Even in the heart of winter, strong design and evergreen plantings make it a place of great and calm beauty. And if snow should fall, it adds just the right emphasis.

At Christmastime in Provence, miniature wintry hilltowns spring up on table tops in every home, re-creating the Nativity scene with figurines called santons. This Provençal tradition dates to the eighteenth century and remains active today through the work of craftspeople who continue to invent new themes and characters.

SANTONS of Provence: The Fair in Arles

In 1223, Saint Francis of Assisi celebrated Christmas by re-enacting the Nativity with live actors. The Christ child alone was carved out of wood, but even he miraculously drew breath when touched by the saint. Thereafter, Nativity scenes, using life-sized statues, became common in churches all over Europe. In the eighteenth century, wealthy families enjoyed small-sized crèches at home, sometimes made of Venetian glass. The fashion for cribs became widespread in Provence when the Revolution closed down the churches after 1793, and the region remained faithful to its religious heritage. At the same time, a craftsman named Jean-Louis Lagnel began to produce crib figurines made of clay, which he sold for pennies. Thus every family could have its *santons,* or little saints, on a tabletop at home, and their manufacture became one of Provence's most appreciated popular arts. The first santon fair took place in Marseilles in 1803,

SANTON Addresses

Always call ahead for an appointment:
Danièle Camargue, 10, rue de Bouillargues, 30128 Garons, Tel: (0) 466 70 14 57.
Elizabeth Ferriol, 4, rue du 4 septembre, 13200 Arles, Tel: (0) 490 93 37 60.
Paul Fouque (Meilleur Ouvrier de France), 65, cours Gambetta, 13100 Aix-en-Provence, Tel: (0) 442 26 33 38.
Laurent Bourges, route de Maillane, Saint-Rémy-de-Provence, Tel: (0) 490 92 20 45.
Colette and Julien Dévouassoux, Puyvert, 84160 Cadenet, Tel: (0) 490 68 02 12.

and still continues today. M. F. K. Fisher described it as "jammed with people, pushing and gaping and joking with the vitality that I believe is peculiar to Marseilles."

The story that the santons depict is always the same. It is as if the Nativity took place in a Provençal hilltown. All the village characters bring as offerings to the Christ child whatever they produce: the garlic seller, his garlic; the poultry raiser, her hens; the shepherd, his lambs. Today, most of the figurines are still made of clay, and may be left in their natural earth colors, or be brightly painted or clothed like little dolls. Some, however, are of papier-maché, wood, and even bread dough. Children often make santons for their parents, adding new ones each year. But all over the southern countryside, professionals have evolved personal styles, based on the old traditions.

Every December, a santon fair is held in the medieval cloister of the cathedral of Saint-Trophime in Arles. Its richly sculpted capitals already include three renderings of the Nativity, which are considered among the finest in Europe. Vaulted rooms lend themselves beautifully to the presentation of these colorful folk. One is devoted to amateurs, whose originality frequently provides some surprises. For example, an entire village produces santons using plastic dolls, clothed in fabrics rescued from the public dump! Others use olive wood for their figurines, choose gypsy themes or offer futuristic renditions. Another room is reserved for the Christmas crafts of a guest country. But

Stone and vegetation are ever mingling in Provence, even in winter, where the tracery of a vine growing up a wall repeats the patterns of a sculpted coat of arms.

On Saint Lucy's day
(December 13), the
days lengthen by a
flea's leap.
A la Sainte-Luce, les jours
augmentent d'un saut
de puce.
A Santo-Lùcio, li jour
aumenton d'un saut
de clusso.

the heart of the exhibit remains the professional show, which every season pays homage to a different master santon maker.

Each fair celebrates a different type of santon: musicians, for example. Today it is fashionable to create village settings for the figurines, much like those crafted for old model-train sets. Indeed, an enormous display of this sort is open year round in Arles, next to the tourist office and the Hôtel Jules César. Taped music, poetry and commentary explain each scene as it is highlighted.

Santons are a wonderful introduction to Christmas in Provence, combining the color, the humor, the love of storytelling with a deep appreciation for rural tradition and for work well done. The scene they depict is still enacted live in the village *pastourales*. Among the many village types represented, a young girl appears, decorated with fine jewelry (in reality, she wears olive-leaf eardrops and grass rings on her fingers). The other villagers mock her, but she replies that the child is far more beautiful than she, and that her ornaments will be her offering. They comment with the typical skepticism of Provençal folk humor: "That's a surer sign than the star! If he can make coquettes sacrifice their finery, he really must be a savior!"

Unfortunately, the santons do not speak. But as one poet commented, in their rich array they constitute the flowers of the winter season.

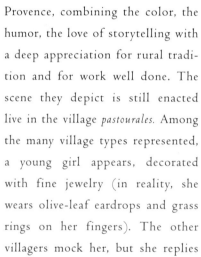

LEFT: *An eerie, rocky landscape, inhabited since prehistoric times, surrounds the medieval castle and hilltown of Les Baux.* OPPOSITE: *Cypresses, like soldiers, guard tiny oak-leaf lettuce on a winter morning.*

Oustau de Baumanière

[Oustau de Baumanière, Les Baux, 13520 Les Baux de Provence.
Tel: (0) 490 97 33 07; FAX: (0) 490 54 40 46.
E-mail: oustau@relaischateaux.fr.
Owner and chef: Jean-André Charial.]

In 1884, Henry James visited Les Baux and admired "the crags of Provence; they are beautifully modeled, as painters say, and they have a delightful silvery color. The road winds round the foot of the hills on the top of which Les Baux is planted . . . the pleasure of climbing into this queerest of cities on foot is not the least part of the entertainment of going there. Then you appreciate its extraordinary position, its picturesqueness, its steepness, its desolation and decay. It hangs—that is, what remains of it—to the slanting summit of the mountain." The writer concluded sadly that "the empty shells of a considerable number of old houses, many of which must have been superb, the lines of certain steep little streets, the foundations of a castle, and ever so many splendid views, are all that remain today. . . ."

Before falling into such ruin and neglect, this famous hilltown had known many brilliant destinies: Once inhabited by cave dwellers, it housed a great lineage of medieval robber barons before being given, as a recompense for loyal services, to the Grimaldi family (the Prince of Monaco still holds the title of Marquis des Baux) by Louis XIV. But its advanced decay was dramatically reversed just after World War II by a new great "lord" of Les Baux, Raymond Thuilier, who transformed an old olive mill at the foot of the hills into the restaurant that has since become a gastronomical mecca. The village above sprung to life again, and

LEFT: *Winter reveals the bare bones of the landscape in all their austere beauty.*

BELOW: *Terraced orchards, fresh-tilled, stand out against the evergreen garrigue, topped by the medieval keep at Suzette.*

Thuilier has served as its mayor for many years. He has even won fame as an artist—all the china and linens used at Baumanière are of his design. The menu cover, however, is the work of a colleague—Jean Cocteau, who dedicated it "To my friend Thuilier, 1959."

Many famous guests, including the Queen of England, have enjoyed the subtle flavors, smooth service and old Provençal decor of this haven, protected by its narrow valley and dominated by the rugged cliffs of the town. One summer, when forest fires from the surrounding slopes threatened the restaurant, French national radio announced the danger to the entire country, which held its breath. Luckily, Baumanière was spared.

Today, although over 90, the patriarch still receives his guests with gracious dignity. But Jean-André Charial, Thuilier's grandson and successor, has developed new areas of interest—including Baumanière's extensive vegetable gardens. These produce, for example, the tiniest and most succulent of green beans, which even the famous wholesale market gardens of the area cannot supply. Monsieur Charial has captured the spirit of the gardens in his published collection of recipes and quotations entitled *A Bouquet from Provence* (Pavillon Books). The restaurant offers a tempting, meatless garden menu that is based on its own produce. A typical example might be:

Winter vegetables and fruits—persimmons, leeks, broccoli and many kinds of greens for salads—add color both to the landscape and the table. Shrubby rosemary flowers all winter long.

> *Vegetable soup of the day*
> *Wild mushrooms in puff pastry*
> *Artichoke mousse*
> *Charlotte of eggplant with sweet pepper sauce*
> *Pear delight and local-fruit tart*

As the days increase,
    so does the cold.
A mesure que les jours
    croissent, le froid
    augmente.
Janvié creissènt,
    fre couiènt.

Baumanière's regular winter menu may well feature the following chicken dish. It is often preceded by a salad of artichoke hearts with cod fritters or truffle ravioli with leeks. Either a white Châteauneuf-du-Pape wine or a Château Simone, powerful and supple enough to accommodate the strong flavors of the main course, would make an excellent accompaniment. Afterward, dessert can be chosen from the restaurant's fabulously laden cart, or, if something hot, such as a tart of spiced pears, is preferred, it can be ordered at the beginning of the meal.

On clear days, the Mont Ventoux, with its observatory tower, can be seen dominating even highly perched villages such as Methamis.

Chicken Breast with Rosemary and Anchovy

▲▲▲▲▲▲▲▲▲▲▲▲▲▲▲▲▲▲▲▲▲▲▲

Serves 2

3½-pound chicken

3 anchovy fillets in oil (unsalted)

STOCK

Chicken carcass

2 teaspoons butter

¼ pound mushrooms, cleaned and chopped

2 carrots, scraped and sliced

2 onions, peeled and chopped

1 celery stalk, cleaned and chopped

1 small leek, cleaned and chopped (the white part and a small section of the green)

1 clove garlic, peeled and chopped

1 cup white wine

2 cups cold water (or enough to cover the carcass in the pan)

SAUCE

2½ cups chicken stock

2 cups heavy cream

Branch of rosemary, fresh if possible, or 1 teaspoon dried rosemary

Salt

Pepper

1 tablespoon butter

Prepare the chicken: Remove the wings and skin with a sharp boning knife. Make two deep cuts next to the backbone, on either side, to loosen the breasts. They should come off easily with two further incisions at the point where the wings were removed. Cut off the rest of the meat from the chicken and reserve for another purpose. Only the carcass will be needed to prepare the stock.

This dish can also be made with chicken breasts (about ½ pound each) if you have bones left over from another meal for making the stock.

Make 3 small incisions in each chicken breast, then insert half an anchovy fillet into each. Cover the breasts and refrigerate while making the stock.

Prepare the chicken stock: Break the carcass into pieces and flatten with a cleaver. Melt the butter in a large pot, then add the carcass pieces and brown. Add the vegetables and stir. Pour in the white wine and the water. Bring the mixture to a boil and simmer, uncovered, for an hour. Skim off any particles that have risen to the surface and strain. There will be enough stock left for another recipe.

Prepare the sauce: Pour 2 cups of the stock into a saucepan with the cream and the branch of rosemary. Reduce the liquid, uncovered, simmering for about 40 minutes, or until thick. Remove the rosemary branch (or strain if dried rosemary is used). Season to taste.

For the final preparation: In a sauté pan, melt the butter, then add the chicken breasts. Brown lightly on both sides. Add the remaining ½ cup stock and simmer gently for 15 minutes.

Arrange the chicken breasts in the center of a platter, ladle some sauce over them and surround with steamed broccoli or other colorful vegetable.

ABOVE: Tambourins *(drums)* *are among the traditional* *Provençal instruments made* *by Jean-Pierre Magnan.* OPPOSITE: *Frosty winter light* *magically highlights an aban-* *doned shed and orchard.*

Ancient Music

[Jean-Pierre Magnan, 8b, rue de Mazeau, 84100 Orange. *Tel: (0) 490 34 25 62. Situated in back of the municipal museum in* *Orange, with a separate entrance. The antiques shop is open 8 A.M. to* *12 P.M. and 2 P.M. to 7 P.M. and Saturday mornings. To visit the* *furniture and instrument workshops, an appointment is necessary.]*

The Magnans have been makers of fine furniture for four generations. Jean-Pierre, however, creates musical instruments in precious woods and ivory. Naturally, he concentrates on the local specialties, the *galoubet* (similar to a fife or a recorder) and the *tambourin* (a long drum). But eight other old instruments are also available.

A galoubet is made of boxwood, tropical woods or ebony. A drum, which can be beautifully sculpted, consists of a hollow walnut cylinder with the skin of a stillborn calf stretched over the top end, and deerskin over the bottom. Decoration, which might include a coat of arms and floral motifs (similar to that of Louis XVI furniture) can take 40 hours to complete.

Traditionally, one man would play both instruments, using one hand for each, as he walked in a parade or accompanied a folk dance. First made in Provence between the tenth and twelfth centuries, these instruments most likely did not originate in the Midi. It is known that they were once used to play folk music in countries as far apart as Argentina and Belgium. Imported into Mexico by Spaniards, they later became popular during the American Revolution. Antique Provençal versions can be seen in the Arlatan Museum in Arles and the Château d'Ambert, near Marseilles.

Monsieur Magnan's main customers are lovers of ancient music, folk groups and curious musicians. Their interest is

Vines in winter create intricate and unexpected patterns that foliage hides for most of the year. Often used for trellising because they leaf out late, they provide shade only when the weather has turned hot.

not, he insists, a mere survival of folk-lore, but the active continuity of a lively tradition of popular music.

The manufacture of musical instruments and furniture is housed in the vaults of an old priory (the work-shop was once the kitchen). Monsieur Magnan produces bedsteads, wardrobes, even grandfather clocks with the same elab-orately sculpted motifs that were fashion-able in the eighteenth century. There is always an apprentice at the Magnan workshop, as the craft can be learned only through practical experience. The time involved, however, makes produc-tion too costly to attract too many new devotees. Fortunately, there is a young Magnan willing to take on the family business in the next generation.

Food with the Famous in Arles IV: Rebirth

After 1970, the Hôtel Nord-Pinus in Arles went into decline. Despite bankruptcy, Germaine clung tenaciously to her once-illustrious establishment. But by 1987, when she died, she had become a kind of squatter on decaying premises, owning only the wrought-iron banister of the stairwell and the precious guest book with its sketch by Paul Klee.

In the late 1980s, the Place du Forum in the heart of Arles

February snows last as
long as water in a
basket. February snows,
poor man's manure.

Neige de février ne tient
pas plus que l'eau
dans un panier. Neige
de février, fumier
du pauvre.

Nèu de febrié tèn pas
mai que l'aigo dins
un panié. Nèu de
febrié fumié.

underwent a great facelift. It acquired new custom in the patrons of Arles's now internationally known summer photography festival. Just days before her death, Germaine relinquished her interest in the Hôtel Nord-Pinus to a new owner, Anne Igou—a young Midi woman of the sort so much admired by centuries of travelers. Germaine had refused many previous offers but found comfort, perhaps, in selling to another woman, something of a Bohemian like herself.

Perhaps Germaine sensed that Madame Igou would draw to the Nord-Pinus yet another swirling world of famous patrons. And so it has proved to be—but this new public comes from the sphere of high fashion. After a complete revamping of the premises done with "fantaisie" and "simplicité" (key words in Madame Igou's vocabulary), the first arrivals were photographers from *Vogue.* Couturiers like Christian Lacroix, who is from Arles, became patrons and admirers. Designer Inès de la Fressange was married at the hotel. Sophisticated blow-ups by Anne's "copain," fashion photographer Peter Lindberg, decorate the lobby.

The Nord-Pinus today has become a youthful, free-wheeling, good-humored place, run along quite unconventional lines. Madame Igou may herself park cars or check plumbing. She values spontaneity and makes up her timetable as she goes along. And her charm and warmth infuse the whole place. The famous flock here still, and film crews regularly invade the place.

The Nord-Pinus today has a colorful bistro dining room, but much of its food is served outdoors on the bustling Place du Forum. Its cuisine has taken a marked change for the better, thanks to a creative partnership between Madame Igou and the legendary restaurant, the Oustau de Baumanière. Chef Jérôme Federighi works here under the direction of Jean-André Charial, who can experiment in Arles with more home-style cuisine than many customers would accept at Baumanière.

The Hôtel Nord-Pinus in Arles combines an illustrious heritage with a markedly improved cuisine.

A CHICK-PEA FABLE

Two Marseilles sailors promised during a storm at sea to climb the hundreds of steps leading to Notre-Dame-de-la-Garde, high above the city, with chick-peas in their shoes. They were spared.

But chick-peas are hard, and have pointed little beaks like donkey horns. Walking half an hour uphill with them in your shoes can be hard on the feet.

One of the sailors was straining, limping and lamenting, while the other remained serene. So much so that in the end, his friend asked him how he managed. Easy, replied the other, I cooked them first. Frédéric Mistral, ALMANACH 1872

A typical set menu at the Nord-Pinus today might include drinks served with country bread and excellent olive oil that has been frozen just long enough to stay spreadable; an eggplant charlotte with red pepper sauce; slices from a tiny leg of lamb served with snow peas and potatoes, and a light savory-flavored sauce; finally, a poached pear with caramel, honey and almonds.

Anne Igou refuses to get caught up in gastronomic pretension. Most of her friends have never heard of Baumanière, she says. For that very reason, she loves to invite them there. She once hosted at Baumanière two lighthouse-keepers of decidedly modest means. On another occasion, it was a family with children who refused to even consider eating pigeon, knowing it only a as pest from the Place du Forum.

Today the Hôtel Nord-Pinus is still a cosmopolitan crossroads. Its bistro's cooking offers an elegant version of the earthy fare that Mistral and Courtine finally discovered and enjoyed, that Van Gogh yearned for and that M. F. K. Fisher anticipated in vain.

Classical Elegance:
The Château de Barbentane

[Château de Barbentane, 13570 Barbentane. Tel: (0) 490 95 51 07. Château visits Easter to Nov. 1, every day except Wednesday: 10:00 A.M. to 12 P.M.; 2:00 P.M. to 6:00 P.M. In winter, Sundays only. Gardens only may be seen as part of the château visit. Private property of Henri de Puget de Barbentane.]

Southwest of Avignon lies the charming town of Barbentane, where a typical maze of medieval streets settles against a cliff topped by a public promenade.

That year winter was hard, the ice had never been
so thick on the stream. Never had we felt such cold, so
bitter that it froze the wind in the depths of the sky.
The whole country shivered in silence. The grazing slopes
above the village were all silvered over. There was not a
cloud in the sky. Every morning, a rusty ball rose in
silence, took three careless giant steps across the heavens
and disappeared. Night heaped up the stars like grain.
Jean Giono, REGAIN

ABOVE: *The long north terrace of the château of Barbentane has a rococco balustrade, sheltered under canopies of redbud trees and century-old planes.*
ABOVE RIGHT: *The tight pinkish-red buds of laurustinus are highly decorative; when the flowers open to pinkish-white in mid-winter, their fragrance carries some distance.* RIGHT: *At Barbegal, the Romans constructed a sophisticated hydraulic plant, the ruins of which now look down on the geometries of winter fields below.*

On a back road stands one of the few extant windmills of Provence that has kept its sails. A ruined tower in the old town can be seen from all sides; it is where an Avignon pope took refuge in the fourteenth century, during the plague.

In 1443, the Good King René ennobled a local family, ancestors of today's château owners. In 1654, Jean de Puget bought land on the edge of town, and his grandson began construction of the château 20 years later. An eighteenth-century descendant returned after years as ambassador to Tuscany to complete the interior decoration, which is ornate and reflects both Parisian and Italian influences. This mini-Versailles has remained undamaged throughout all the vagaries of history, keeping its original furniture, and has stayed in the original family's possession. No doubt the ancestor who served as a general in the Revolutionary army did his part to preserve the family heritage.

Inside, Florentine marble decors and Venetian chandeliers complement a series of flat-vaulted stone ceilings, which were the specialty of a gifted local architect. Family portraits; pirate chests; hand-painted eighteenth-century wallpapers, with matching fabrics; and rare enameled commodes are among the priceless treasures displayed. One reception room has its own, specially ordered Louis xv furniture, including a pair of matching, asymmetrical couches. Each piece is covered with embroidered tapestries depicting La Fontaine fables. Their woodwork is painted black, probably as a sign of mourning after the beheading of Louis xvi. Photographed countless times, the château interior served also as decor for a television serial based on the popular novels called *Les Gens de Mogador*.

Outside, little remains of the château's original neoclassical gardens, relandscaped in the nineteenth century.

On New Year's Day, the days lengthen by a cock's meal.

Au jours de l'an, les jours croissent du repas d'un coq.

Oou jou de l'an, lei jou creissoun doou repas d'un can.

Winter vineyards against the austere, windswept slopes of the Alpilles hills look like some mysterious script on the landscape.

Outside the mistral purred. In the slowly thawing gardens were the memorable flaccid palms in their circles of molting grass. There was still snow-rime in the flowerbeds.
Lawrence Durrell,
MONSIEUR

When the mistral blows here, the countryside is anything but welcoming for this wind is extremely irritating. But, on the other hand, how wonderful when it stops, what intensity of color, what pure air, what supreme luminosity.
Vincent Van Gogh,
COLLECTED LETTERS

The oriental planes, which now soar high above the southern esplanade, were grown from seeds brought back from Italy by the ambassador ancestor. Also from the past is a unique series of garden sculptures; those on the balustrade combine eighteenth-century elegance and wit in a most appealing manner.

Visitors are welcome at Barbentane and are shown around by efficient, trained guides every half hour. But there is never, even at the height of the season, a hurried atmosphere. And, occasionally, those waiting their turn may come upon the Marquis pruning his roses.

The "Mud-Eater" Mistral

One of the popular *santons* of Provence is an angel with puffed, round cheeks, who hangs above the manger scene, blowing for all he is worth. This is the angel *Boufarèu*, or "mud-eater," who is also represented in stone above the monumental stairwell of the Château de Barbentane. The cold north blast he blows with such force is the famous mistral, a term derived from the Latin word *magister*, meaning "force," and which quite independently gave rise also to the family name Mistral.

The mistral does, indeed, dry up mud, clearing skies almost instantly—qualities so appreciated by the philosopher Nietzsche that he composed a song in its praise. For him, it becomes a symbol of all that chases gloom away: "Mistral wind, hunter of clouds, death of grief, purity of heaven, How I love your roaring. . . . On slippery, rocky paths, I run, dancing, to greet you. . . ." His sentiments are

God give us joy, god give
us joy,
Christmas is coming,
May God's grace ensure,
in the coming year
That if we are not more,
we may not be fewer.

Chant recited together by
the oldest and youngest
members of the family
during the Christmas
Eve ceremony of the
CACHO-FIO, when an olive
branch which has been
dipped in mulled wine is
used to anoint the yule
log. Thus human growth
and that of the land are
linked in prayer.

not generally shared by the local populace, however. The mistral has the reputation of getting on one's nerves. Marie Mauron, a writer of the Alpilles region, records her mixed feelings about "the blue wind, the drunken wind which intoxicates people with its drunkenness, enervates animals, maddens flowers, plants, trees, the very sky even as it sand-papers it to a hardness. It sings strong and loud, with hoarse throaty noises of excitement at the game . . . Aerial Rhone which is the river of our sky. . . . The Provençaux say that you do too much ill to speak well of you and too much good to speak ill. But this judgement says nothing of the virile beauty of your song."

Terracing on steep hillsides traditionally provides wind protection
and helps prevent soil erosion.

This dry north or northwest wind builds force in the funnel of the Rhone Valley whenever pres-sure mounts over the mountains on either side. Folklore claims that it blows in cycles of three days, at least if it starts up by daylight. Rising by night, it may last only "the time it takes to bake bread," according to a regional proverb.

Recently, a group of Provençal schoolchildren partici-pated in a survey. Asked what they would put on a poster to represent Provence, they all suggested landscapes: the wild *garrigue*, with its thyme, lavender and rosemary, cica-das, green oaks, pines and olive trees. Some mentioned cul-tivated orchards and old habitations—farmhouses, villages and the vaulted stone dwellings called *bories*—under an eternally blue sky. But they all agreed that it would be best not to mention the mistral!

Generations of Candy Making: The Jouvaud Family

[Confiseries Jouvaud, rue de l'Evêché, 84200 Carpentras.
Tel: (0) 490 63 15 38; FAX: (0) 490 63 21 62.
E-mail: jouvauddesserts@avignon.pacwan.]

Candied fruit and delicate pastries are prepared in small batches with the best ingredients by the Jouvaud family in Carpentras.

In the medieval center of the town of Carpentras, near the public market, not far from the cathedral of Saint-Siffrein, one shop window is so beautifully arranged, so colorful in its array, that it seems almost like a gallery. And so it is, although most of its wares are edible: Here, the Jouvaud family—parents and children—sells candy and pastries of great elegance and refinement. On the walls hang watercolors by Monsieur Jouvaud senior, representing local rural landscapes at different seasons.

The older Monsieur Jouvaud apprenticed in the candy business with a descendant of the man who, in 1850, invented the famous Carpentras specialty, the *berlingot*, a mint-flavored sweet reputed to cure all ills. Now the younger generation has transformed the shop into a small tearoom, decorated with local fabrics and carefully chosen pottery, much of which is also for sale.

Candied fruit was once a regional specialty in Carpentras, as it still is in Apt, where, however, most of the candy makers have become industrialized (heavily polluting the local rivers). In their factories, fruit is stored in vats of chemical solutions until there is enough to process it in large batches. Jouvaud, on the other hand, makes very small quantities at a time, always with fresh

fruit that is just ripe—pears, melons, prunes, cherries. As for apricots, he uses an old-fashioned variety called "rose de Provence," which a local farmer grows solely for him. For chocolate-covered cherries, he seeks out the sour variety that is rarely seen in the public markets because of its modest appearance. For quince buns, a local specialty in which the fruit is baked in bread dough, he selects quinces from un-watered hedges, because their flavor is much more intense. Aware of his customers' preference for confections that are less sweet than formerly, Jouvaud uses only half the amount of pure cane sugar that his father did 20 years ago. He takes great care with his methods, explaining, "You can't really cheat even if you wanted to, the old ones are always watching."

So are the young, it would seem. There is now a six-year-old Jouvaud who, at this tender age, is undecided about his future. The elder Monsieur Jouvaud took his grandson to Flassans last fall, where they planted a patch of wheat. Grand-father and grandchild tended it through the growing season, harvested it in June, threshed it and ground about two pounds of flour. With this, they made tea cakes (*madeleines*), much to the boy's delight. And so the family looks to its future. . . .

Christmas breads and deep-fried oreillettes *are featured during the festive season; but the Jouvauds imagine new creations every month for celebrations all year round.*

No child nor adult can resist the subtle flavors of the Jouvaud specialties: the Saint Siffrein, for example, with its caramelized walnuts and its blend of soft and crackly chocolate; the lemon cake, with its hidden layer of praline; or the chocolate truffles, with three kinds of chocolate. The Jouvauds invent one new cake a month for the pleas-ure of their regular customers, and also furnish chocolates to such fine hotels as the Hostellerie de Crillon-le-Brave.

Although the Jouvauds mail their confections all over the world, it is worth visiting the shop for its beautiful displays and happy atmosphere.

CURNONSKY'S STEWED TRUFFLES

Watching wily truffle dealers on winter mornings at the Friday market of Carpentras (northeast of Avignon) is one of the best local sports.

"Proust conjures up Combray," says the great chef Curnonsky, "its panorama and its good people, from a teacake dipped in a cup of herb tea. An exiled citizen of Carpentras could call into being his native town, with its monuments and all the resources of its countryside, as in a dream, from a truffle stew.

"You must find local truffles the size of an honest potato. Brush them. Peel them. Crush the peelings with a little olive oil in a mortar and strain the mixture through a sieve. Slice your truffles into scallops and put them to cook gently in an earthenware pot, with a carrot, the white part of one leek,

Historical Pastries

[Anne Daguin, Le Petit Duc: pâtisseirs, fabricants de douceurs. 7 boulevard Victor Hugo, 13210 Saint-Rémy-de-Provence. Tel: and FAX: (0) 490 92 08 31.]

Anne Daguin creates historical pastries at Le Petit Duc, in Saint-Rémy-de-Provence. Not only are they delicious, but they are also Roman or Renaissance, Alpine or Arlesian, recipes culled from archives of all periods.

As a food historian, Anne always wants to know the how and why of her ingredients. Sugar, for example, in the Middle Ages was reserved for the very wealthy, and for medicinal use only. Nostradamus, a doctor and astronomer who lived in Saint-Rémy at the Renaissance, experimented with new techniques for cooking sugar, seeking ways of preserving summer's fruits for winter— dried, as jam, or as the candied fruit that is still such a specialty of the region today. But these old recipes give no idea of times or quantities. Anne and her husband become pastry detectives in their attempts to reconstitute them. It took them six months to develop "pignolat," a mixture of sugar, pine nuts, rose water and fennel.

Anne is half Provençal, half Gascon. Her husband and partner in pastry, Hermann Van Beeck, is German-Flemish. Anne remembers that Provence, in all its rich history, has always been a crossroads, that even the tomato was once an exotic import, that Nostradamus himself learned much from the Ottoman fleet that, in the sixteenth century, wintered in Toulon. Her work exemplifies all that is best in this cosmopolitan but authentically Provençal tradition.

an onion, thyme, bayleaf, all chopped very fine; add also your puréed peelings and some thickened veal broth. During the cooking, lengthen with a glass of Châteauneuf-du-Pape, and serve up, placing each slice on a triangle of fried bread."

OPPOSITE: *A terra-cotta fisherman is displayed among the many treasures at Sud Restauration, east of Carpentras.* ABOVE: *A young enthusiast presents a fine selection of truffles at the Friday-morning market in Carpentras.*

PUMPKIN SOUP WITH LEEK GARNISH

Serves 6

2 large leeks, white and small
  section of green, cleaned
  and minced
4 tablespoons butter
1 large onion, peeled and minced
1 clove garlic, peeled and minced
2 pounds pumpkin or winter
  squash, peeled and cubed
Pinch of grated nutmeg
2 cups heavy cream
2 tablespoons vegetable oil
1 clove unpeeled garlic
5 slices fresh white bread,
  crusts removed, cubed
2 tablespoons flat parsley
  or chervil

Place one of the minced leeks in a bowl of cold water and set aside for use as garnish. In a large saucepan, melt 2 tablespoons butter over high heat, and when foaming, add the remaining leek, the onion and minced garlic. Lower the heat and cook gently, without browning, for 5 minutes, or until just barely soft. Add the cubed pumpkin and nutmeg, and turn well to coat with butter. Cover the pan and simmer the mixture for about

Christian Etienne: A City Chef Who Loves Vegetables

[Christian Etienne, 10, rue de Mons, 84000 Avignon. Tel: (0) 490 86 16 50; FAX: (0) 490 86 67 09. E-mail: christian.etienne.resto@wanadoo.fr. Web: www.avignon-et-provence.com.]

Christian Etienne belongs to Avignon, and, nowadays, Avignon to Christian Etienne. Few local sons have won such a strong and loyal following; his is due primarily to the rigor and originality of his cuisine, but also, perhaps, to the extraordinary setting of his restaurant—it is housed in the only private dwelling to be linked by a stone arch to the massive fourteenth-century Papal Palace for which Avignon is famous. Period frescoes and a painted ceiling were discovered during extensive restoration work, and provide an incomparable decor.

A city man, Christian Etienne spent some years working in Paris, notably at the Ritz. But when his car was impounded for illegal parking twice in one day, he began to think longingly of his native Avignon. He returned to open a tiny bistrot, and it did not take long for the avid local clientele to discover him. One of his customers mentioned that an abandoned property in the center of town was for sale. Strangely, Monsieur Etienne's mother remembers taking her son to the public gardens on a nearby hill when he was only four years old, and swears that, even at such a tender age, he pointed out this very building to her, saying, "Someday I will buy that house, Maman."

So his prediction has come true; his restaurant opened in 1990. But in Provence, city and country are inextricably linked, and no one knows better than Monsieur Etienne how

30 minutes, turning often.

Provençal pumpkin gives off quite a bit of liquid, whereas American squash, of a denser texture, may need a few tablespoons of water added. Continue simmering (uncovered, if very liquid) for about 20 minutes longer, or until evenly cooked through. Stir in the cream and simmer for another 20 minutes. Pour the soup into a food processor or blender and process to a smooth consistency. Return to the saucepan and keep hot.

Prepare the croutons: In a sauté pan, melt 1 tablespoon of butter with 1 tablespoon of oil and the unpeeled garlic. Add the bread cubes and cook, turning often, until the croutons are evenly golden. Set them aside.

Prepare the leek garnish: Remove the minced leek from the water and drain well. In a sauté pan, melt 1 tablespoon of butter with 1 tablespoon of oil and cook the minced leek until the shreds become just crispy and brown.

Serve the soup hot, garnished with the leek shreds, croutons and a sprinkling of parsley.

Monsieur Pitot's faience draws on the craft traditions of Apt, but his tableware is recognizable all over the region as distinctively his own.

COUNTRY DECOR: THE FAÏENCE OF APT

[Antony Pitot, Quartier de Ponty, R.N. 100, 84200 Goult. Tel: (0) 490 72 22 79. Visits by appointment only]

Monsieur Pitot has made quite a reputation for himself as a successful creator of the glazed earthenware.

to follow the seasons to ensure the absolute freshness of all his food. Simplicity is his hallmark; he always seeks to bring out the best flavors of the natural ingredients he uses, without the elaborate and mysterious mixtures that once characterized sophisticated cooking. His cuisine reflects his concern for precision with what he calls "feeling," or individual inspiration; in this respect, he is like a musician. As chef, he is both composer and interpreter, and he claims that his exchanges with customers always affect his performance. Many who eat in his restaurant simply leave the menu to his discretion. Sometimes clients will feel like drinking a certain wine, and he will confer with his excellent sommelier, Monsieur Reboul, about creating a menu around this choice. Monsieur Etienne and his staff like to welcome guests as they would to their own homes. Although many owners may make such a claim, the easy and happy mood of those working here ensures that it rings true.

Christian Etienne regularly offers a meatless menu based entirely on seasonal produce. Here, you might encounter a fennel sherbet with saffron sauce or the hard Provençal mountain wheat known as *épeautre.* The recipe, opposite, for pumpkin soup is an excellent example of the chef's inspiration. No dish could be more traditionally Provençal, and yet his version has a subtle refinement all its own. It remains simple, and each ingredient (Monsieur Etienne likes to quote Brillat-Savarin on this score) keeps the taste of what it is.

known as FAIENCE. He draws on the country traditions surrounding Apt, where the familiar ocher tones and greens of Provençal pottery elsewhere were further enriched by a special marbling effect called JASPAGE, which catches the light most decoratively. Monsieur Pitot's colors are obtained by using white clay tinted in the mass with copper oxides. Enameled without lead, his tableware can be used every day—and is much sought after by those who seek to create Provence country decors. The elaborate cakes produced at the Pâtisserie in Villeneuve-lez-Avignon are displayed on his crockery. Reasonably priced, it ranges from small cups and butter dishes to elaborate assemblages of brightly colored fruit on platters to baskets with fretwork as fine as lace.

*A mon Caillat —
Londres 24 juin 1902
A. Escoffier*

MENU

Caviar Frais   Melon Cantaloup

Consommé aux Nids d'Hirondelle

Velouté Royale

Mousseline d'Ecrevisses

Poularde Edouard VII.

Noisettes d'Agneau Régence

Suprèmes de Caneton

Neige au Clicquot

Ortolans au Suc d'Ananas

Cœurs de Romaine aux Fines Herbes

Artichauts Favorite

Pêches Alexandra

Mon Désir   Mignardises

GALA DINNER.

CARLTON RESTAURANT JUNE 1902

QUOTATIONS FROM
AUGUSTE
ESCOFFIER'S
*MEMORIES OF
MY LIFE*

*(Excerpts by permission from the
Escoffier family, translated by
Laurence Escoffier. The Culinary
Institute of America. New York:
Van Nostrand Reinhold, 1997.)*

WOMEN'S CUISINE

Noting the excellence of French resources, Escoffier concludes, "It is therefore only natural that French men have become both gourmets and fine chefs.

"But for a population to enjoy fine cuisine, it is also important that they should have had a long heritage of a courteous style of living that stresses the importance of a good meal celebrated among friends, and that there should be a strong domestic tradition whereby all the secrets of fine cooking are transmitted from mother to daughter...."

An Escoffier souvenir menu in Villeneuve-Loubet.

Escoffier Our Contemporary

[Musée de l'Art culinaire—Fondation Auguste Escoffier—Institut Joseph Donon, 06270 Villeneuve-Loubet (Village). Tel: (0) 493 20 80 51; FAX: (0) 493 73 93 79. Open from 2 P.M. to 6 P.M. summers every day but Monday and holidays. Closed in November.]

Food lovers all over the world know Auguste Escoffier (1846–1935) as a pioneer in the art and science of gastronomy. He was born in this charming house in the old town of Villeneuve-Loubet, just northwest of Nice. Like most Provençal village houses, it is narrow and high with several stories. Escoffier's father was a smithy, and the iron ring to which horses were tied up to be shod still hangs by the front door. Nearby is a statue of Saint Fortunat: The chef revered him as patron saint of cooks and celebrated his feast day, on December 13, with great banquets every year. Inside, you will find not only a wide array of mementos of Escoffier's brilliant career but also the fireplace where his mother cooked and a rustic Provençal dining room table set for a meal. Among the documents is a menu signed by opera star Nellie Melba, for whom Escoffier invented his famous peach dessert.

Escoffier began working at his uncle's restaurant in Nice at the age of thirteen and later served for decades as chef at the Grand Hotel in Monte Carlo and the Savoy and Carleton hotels in London. He was the first chef to become widely respected as a great artist and a cosmopolitan media star, the first to receive the Legion of Honor. But many imagine this man as something of a relic—to be revered, of course, but belonging to another, fussier age. Escoffier's memoirs, however, reveal how farsighted he was, surprisingly contemporary in his comments. They bear witness to a philosophy and practice still appropriate for today's cooks.

AGAINST THE PUFF AND PRETENSION OF HAUTE CUISINE

"Whiting has a bad reputation it does not merit. Its flesh is excellent for the health, light, flaky and not too moist...If whiting had a fancy name like 'starfish' it would be declared the king of fish."

THE NEED FOR SIMPLICITY

After World War I, Escoffier wrote, "The luxurious and prodigious lifestyle that we knew will die, leaving in its wake a period when thrift will be absolutely necessary, as well as a return to simplicity. But this simplicity can be one of good taste, excluding neither the savory perfection of our cuisine nor the correct elegance of our service."

NEED FOR LIGHTER CUISINE

"I often heard that *haute cuisine* was in a state of decadence...far from falling into decadence, the art of cooking was growing and becoming finer every day. It is true that our stomachs do not have the same capacity to eat that they seemed to have in days gone by, but we chefs are here to take care of the necessary changes and adapt ourselves to evolving customs."

NEED FOR FASTER PACING

"Current fashion and habits are such that one can only spend one hour, or an hour and a half, at any single meal."

AGAINST SMOKING

"Not only do people smoke after dinner, which is deplorable enough, but people even smoke during meals. These meals where people smoke while eating should be baptized 'dinner à la nicotine.' It is obvious that every dish from the appetizer to the dessert must have the same disagreeable taste."

Herbal Remedies
for Colds and Flus

The almond, a fine tree, offers the bees their second flowering after the boxwood. In our mountainous country of the Haute-Provence, it starts flowering in late February. At that time, it lights up the entire countryside with its pink or white bouquets. I love to sit beneath an almond tree, with my back against its trunk. A perfumed music envelops me—the hum of the honeybees hard at work, mingled with the gently wafted scent of the flowers.
Marcel Scipion, MEMOIRS OF A BEE SHEPHERD

Provence has long been celebrated for its pungent aromatics, whose essences concentrate within themselves the intensity of the southern sun. Many of the most famous herbs are evergreen—sage, rosemary, the entire group of thymes and savories—while others take the bulbous form, such as garlic, onions, leeks.

The people of Provence are indeed fortunate to have such a wide range of herbs and vegetables to help them combat the ills of winter. Each plant has its traditional claims to health-giving properties, but none more so than garlic (*Allium sativum*). Modern medicine has confirmed its capacity to stimulate circulation and digestive secretions, as well as to protect the respiratory system.

Garlic is also an acknowledged antiseptic. It contains a sulfur oil that releases its vapor when a clove is crushed. If the smell pleases, it can be used to disinfect the air and clear the lungs and the bronchial tubes. One source recommends macerating peeled, crushed cloves in alcohol, then mixing them with milk to mask the taste. Thirty to fifty drops a day of this elixir are said to cure the worst case of bronchitis.

Brilliant persimmons hang from bare branches— precious color in the winter landscape, and fruit for the table that is rich in vitamin C.

AIGO BOLLIDO

▲▲▲▲▲▲▲

Serves 2

1 tablespoon olive oil
1 small leek (the white part
  and the tender green section),
  cleaned and minced
2 cloves garlic, peeled
  and minced
Sprigs of sage and thyme
Branch of fennel
Bay leaf
3 cups freshly boiled water
Salt
Pepper

In a small pan, heat the
olive oil. Add the leek
and garlic, and cook, without browning, until limp.
Add the herbs, then pour
the simmering water over
the mixture. Season,
cover and let sit for about
10 minutes. Remove the
herbs. Reheat the mixture,

There are those with whom garlic disagrees, of course. But for them, it is probably a matter of infrequent consumption rather than disposition. Digestive systems only gradually become accustomed to the strong essence if not born and bred to it. As for its effect on one's breath, garlic seems to linger longer among the uninitiated. Chewing on a fresh coffee bean is thought to help.

A Provençal proverb states that he who has sage in his garden does not need doctors. Antiseptic, like garlic, sage is also reputed to calm the nerves and spasms of coughing or asthma. It can be taken as an infusion, or herb tea, sweetened with honey (steep half an ounce in a quart of water; proportions vary, depending on the freshness of the plant). Or, it can be made into a wine. (Macerate three ounces in a bottle of Port or similar wine for a week, then strain. Take one to three soupspoons after each meal.)

The many thymes and related savories of Provence also provide valuable protection against respiratory infections. When thyme is made into an herb tea, its tannins are effective against coughs. Thyme has long been used to combat infection and encourage the digestive juices. It is also reputed to be aphrodisiac. Its essence "thymol" is highly valued in both the perfume and pharmaceutical industries, and, furthermore, is essential in the production of banknotes!

The most famous and enjoyable winter remedy in Provence is the broth known as "Boiled Water," or *Aigo bollido* (which, according to a local proverb, can save your life!). A cross between a soup and an herb tea, it comes in many versions, varying in complexity from the simplest infusion of sage and garlic, to a vegetable broth, which, with the addition of a poached egg and grated cheese, can become a meal in itself.

but do not boil. Serve warm, inhaling the brew before swallowing.

Variations: Any of the following ingredients can be added to the basic recipe:

A chopped onion can be cooked with the leek and the garlic.

A peeled tomato can be cooked with the leek and garlic, or a tablespoon of tomato sauce added before reheating.

Cooked pasta can be added before reheating.

A poached egg can be added to each person's bowl, before the soup is poured in.

A pinch of saffron can be stirred into the mixture just before serving.

Grated Gruyère cheese can be sprinkled over each person's serving.

Bibliography

Benoit, Fernand. *La Provence et le Comtat Venaissin: arts et traditions populaires*. Avignon: Aubanel, 1975.

Bosco, Henri. *Le Trestoulas*. Paris: Gallimard, 1935.

____. *Le Mas Théotime*. Paris: Gallimard, 1952.

Braudel, Fernand. *L'Identité de la France*. 4 vols. Paris: Arthaud-Flammarion, 1986.

Clébert, Jean Paul. *Almanach Provençal 1984*. Paris: Rivages, 1984.

Colette. *La Vagabonde*. Paris: Albin Michel, 1973.

____. *Prisons et paradis*. Paris: Fayard, 1986.

Conran, Terence. *Terence Conran's France*. London: Conran Octopus, 1987.

Courtine, Robert. "Quest for the Big Aïoli" in *Feasts of a Militant Gastronome*. Translated by June Guicharnaud. New York: William Morrow and Co., 1974.

Daudet, Alphonse. *Lettres de mon moulin*. Paris: Fasquelle, 1970.

Doran, P. M., ed. *Conversations avec Cézanne*. Paris: Editions Macula, 1978.

Durrell, Lawrence. *Monsieur*. Harmondsworth: Penguin, 1984.

____. *Caesar's Vast Ghost*. London: Faber and Faber, 1990.

____. *Livia*. Harmondsworth: Penguin, 1984.

____. *Spirit of Place*. New Haven, Connecticut: Leete's Island Books, 1969.

Escoffier, Auguste. *Memories of My Life*. Translated by Laurence Escoffier. The Culinary Institute of America. New York: Van Nostrand Reinhold, 1997.

Etienne, Christian. *La Magie de la tomate*. Aix-en-Provence: Edisud, 1998.

Fisher, M. F. K. "About Looking Alone at a Place: Arles" in *As They Were*. New York: Alfred A. Knopf, 1982.

____. *Two Towns in Provence*. New York: Vintage Books, 1983.

Forbes, Leslie. *A Taste of Provence*. Boston: Little Brown and Co., 1988.

Ford, Ford Madox. *Provence*. New York: Ecco Press, 1979.

Giono, Jean. *Rondeur des Jours*. Paris: Gallimard, 1969.

____. *Le Chant de la Terre*. Paris: Gallimard, 1969.

____. *Manosque-des-Plateaux suivi de Poème de l'olive*. Paris: Gallimard, 1986.

____. *Regain*. Paris: Gallimard, 1969.

Harant, Hervé and Daniel Jarry. *Guide du naturaliste dans le Midi de la France*. Neuchâtel, Switzerland: Delachaux and Niestlé, 1967.

James, Henry. *A Little Tour in France*. Oxford: Oxford University Press, 1984.

Jones, Louisa. *Gardens of Provence*. Flammarion: New York and Paris, 1992.

____. *Gardens of the French Riviera*. Flammarion: New York and Paris, 1994.

____. *Kitchen Gardens of France*. Albin Michel and Thames and Hudson: London, 1997.

____. *L'Esprit nouveau des jardins en Provence / The New Provençal Garden*. Hachette: Paris, 1998.

____. *The New Provençal Cuisine*. Chronicle Books: San Francisco, 1995.

Jouveau, René. *La Cuisine provençal de tradition populaire*. Nîmes, France: Imprimerie Bene, 1976.

Mauron, Marie. *Le printemps de la Saint Martin*. Paris: Atelier Marcel Julian, 1979.

Mistral, Frédéric. *Dernières proses d'alamanch*. Paris: Bernard Grasset, 1930.

____. *Memoirs*. Translated by George Wickes. New York: Directions, 1988.

Mouriès, Nathalie. *Almanach Provençal 1991*. Paris: Rivages, 1991.

Pagnol, Marcel. *Le Château de ma mère*. Paris: Press Pocket, 1972.

____. *Jean de Florette*. Paris: Editions de Fallois, 1989.

____. *La Gloire de mon père*. Paris: Editions de Fallois, 1988.

____. *Manon des Sources*. Paris: Presse Pocket, 1976.

Pickvance, Ronald. *Van Gogh in Arles*. New York: Metropolitan Museum of Art, 1984.

Pope-Hennessy, James. *Aspects of Provence*. London: Penguin Travel Library, 1988.

Riche, August, ed. *La Provence en Poésie*. Paris: Gallimard Folio Junior, 1986.

Roskill, Mark. *The Letters of Vincent Van Gogh*. New York: Atheneum, 1963.

Scipion, Marcel. *L'homme qui courait après les fleurs: mémoires d'un berger d'abeilles*. Paris: Seghers, 1984.

Semanié provenç au e di païs d'o pèr 1991. Marseille: Tacussel, 1991.

Stone, Irving, ed. *Dear Theo: The Autobiography of Vincent Van Gogh*. New York: Signet, 1987.

Thompson, David. *Petrarch: An Anthology*. New York: Harper & Row, 1971.

Tournier, Michel. *Pétites proses*. Paris: Gallimard Folio, 1986.

Van Gogh, Vincent. *Lettres à Théo*. Paris: Gallimard, 1988.

Wentick, Charles and Lucien Clergue. *Arles Van Gogh*. Arles, France: Editions Bernard Coutaz, 1989.

____. *Provence: Mythes et réalités*. Arles, France: Editions Bernard Coutaz, 1989.

Wickes, George, ed. "Readings for Innocents Abroad." Anthology of photocopied literary excerpts, Avignon, Spring 1985.

Wilkins, Ernest Hatch. *Life of Petrarch*. Chicago and London: Phoenix Books, 1962.

Wylie, Lawrence. *Village in the Vaucluse*. Cambridge: Harvard University Press, 1974.

Yapp, Peter, ed. *The Travellers' Dictionary of Quotations*. London: Routledge and Kegan Paul, 1983.

Photo Credits

Louisa Jones: Front cover (top left and bottom right), back cover, 7 (top), 12 (both), 13, 14, 18-20 (all), 22-24 (all), 25 (left), 26, 28 (left), 29, 32, 33, 35, 36 (left), 37 (right), 38, 40-42 (all), 44-45 (both), 54-56 (all), 58, 61 (top and bottom), 62-63 (both), 66-69 (all), 72, 74, 76, 78, 79 (left), 84, 88 (top left and bottom right), 89 (right), 94-99 (all), 102, 104 (top left), 106-108 (all), 110, 112-113 (all), 116 (both), 117, 122, 123 (both), 125, 126-128, 131, 134, 135 (bottom), 138, 139 (bottom), 140-142 (both), 145, 146 (left), 147, 152, 155 (bottom), 156-157, 159, 162, 165.
Vincent Motte: Front cover (top right and bottom left), 2, 6 (both), 10-11, 30-31 (both), 36-37, 50-51, 52-53, 59, 64, 72-73, 80-81, 83, 84-85, 88-89, 92-93, 100, 101, 103, 104-105, 108-109, 114-115, 118, 120-121, 121 (right), 124, 132-133, 135 (top), 136, 143, 144, 146 (right), 148, 150-151, 154-155, 155 (top), 168.
Philippe Giraud: 3, 7 (bottom), 47, 48, 86, 119, 121 (left), 150 (left), 160-161 (all), 163.

Michel Barberousse: 21, 39, 46, 70.
Raoul Bussy: 28 (right), 139 (top).
Constantine Christofides: 79 (right).
Bernard Dupont, Sr.: 91.
Bernard Dupont, Jr.: Author portrait.
Heather Willings: 111.
Painting on page 17 © **Joseph Bayol**.
Cloth patterns on page 77 are reproduced courtesy of **Olivades Fabrics**.
Fondation Angladon-Dubrujeaud: 25 (right).
Guy Hervais: 43.
Bernard Touillon: 60.
Hôtel Nord-Pinus: 153.
Fondation Auguste Escoffier: 166.

Acknowledgments

The author would like to express warm thanks to the many people whose helpful cooperation made this book possible: to the garden owners, Mademoiselle Bacou, Monsieur de Barbentane, Madame Casalis, Madame Bayol, Monsieur Lafont, and Sir Terence Conran; to the many diligent men and women who perpetuate the traditions of country crafts; to the chefs, particularly Christian Etienne and Jean-André Charial for their patient advice; to the Escoffier family and Pierrette Boissier; to Martin Stein at La Mirande; to George Wickes and Molly Westling for his wonderful translation of Mistral, and their common support; to Marie Lepoitevin for her friendly listening ear; to Monsieur and Madame Jacques Martin-Raget for their good advice; to Monsieur and Madame Michel Barberousse for their good company on restaurant outings.

And, not least, to my publishers: Leslie Stoker, for her enthusiasm, efficiency and willingness to experiment; Jennifer Walsh for her always cheerful efficiency; Barbara Sturman, for setting the type and making it all fit; and freelance designer Adriane Stark, for her imaginative design.

Addresses

Louisa Jones' web site for current activities, food, and gardens in Provence is www.enprovence.com.

To call the following phone and fax numbers from outside France, use the country code 33, followed by 9 digits without the zero. From within France, dial ten digits, including the zero.

GARDENS

ABBAYE DE SAINT-ANDRÉ, 30400 Villeneuve-lez-Avignon. Tel: (0) 490 25 55 95. Open 10 A.M. to 12 P.M. and 2 P.M. to 5 P.M. October to March, in summer until 6 p.m. Closed Mondays. Private property of Mademoiselle Roseline Bacou (page 138).

BAYOL, JOSEPH, Route de Maillane, 13 Saint-Rémy-de-Provence. Tel: (0) 490 92 11 97. Art gallery open on weekends (page 16).

CHARTREUSE DE BONPAS, 84510 Caumont. Southeast of Avignon. Tel: (0) 490 23 09 59; FAX: (0) 490 23 19 97. Private property of Monsieur and Madame Casalis. Wine tasting is possible (page 98).

CHÂTEAU DE BARBENTANE, 13570 Barbentane. Tel: (0) 490 95 51 07. Private property of Henri de Puget de Barbentane. Château visits Easter to Nov. 1 every day but Wednesday, 10 A.M. to 12 P.M., 2 P.M. to 6 P.M. In winter, Sundays only. Gardens may only be seen as part of the château visit (page 154).

HARMAS DE JEAN-HENRI FABRE, five miles northeast of Orange on the D976 road to Nyons, just outside Sérignan le Comtat, 84830 Sérignan le Comtat. Tel: (0) 490 70 00 44. Caretaker: Monsieur Pierre Teocchi (page 58).

HOTELS AND RESTAURANTS

AUBERGE DE NOVES, Route de Châteaurenard, 13550 Noves. Tel: (0) 490 24 28 28; FAX: (0) 490 24 28 00. E-mail: noves@relaischateaux.fr. Owner: M. André Lalleman (page 18).

BISTROT À MICHEL, Grand Rue, 84220 Cabrières d'Avignon. Tel: (0) 490 76 82 08. Owner: Michel Bosc. Chef: Ian Bosc (page 123).

CHÂTEAU DE ROCHEGUDE, 26700 Rochegude. Tel: (0) 475 97 21 10; FAX: (0) 475 04 89 87 (page 107).

CHRISTIAN ETIENNE RESTAURANT, 10, rue de Mons, 84000 Avignon. Closed Sundays all year except July, Sundays, and Mondays, September 15-June 15. E-mail: christian.etienne.resto@wanadoo.fr. Tel: (0) 490 86 16 50; FAX: (0) 490 86 67 09. Web: www.avignon-et-provence.com. (page 164).

HOSTELLERIE DE CRILLON-LE-BRAVE, Place de l'Eglise, 84410 Crillon-le-Brave. Tel: (0) 490 65 61 61; FAX: (0) 490 65 62 86. Owners: Peter Chittick and Craig Miller. E-mail: crillonbrave@relaischateaux.fr. Web: www.crillonlebrave.com (page 69).

LA BONNE ETAPE, Chemin du Lac, 04160 Château Arnoux. Owner and chef: Jany Gleize. E-mail: bonneetape@relaischateaux.fr. Tel: (0) 492 64 00 09; FAX: (0) 492 64 37 37 (page 89).

LA MIRANDE, Place l'Amirande, 84000 Avignon. Tel: (0) 490 85 93 93; FAX: (0) 490 86 26 85. E-mail: mirande@worldnet.net. Web: www.la-mirande.fr. Director: Monsieur Martin Stein (page 42).

NORD-PINUS, Place du Forum, 13200 Arles. Tel: (0) 490 93 44 44; FAX: (0) 490 93 34 00. Owner: Madame Anne Igou (pages 27, 90, 106, 152).

LE PRIEURÉ, 7, Place du Chapitre, 30400 Villeneuve-lez-Avignon, across the Rhône from Avignon. Tel: (0) 490 15 90 15; FAX: (0) 490 25 45 39. E-mail: leprieure@avignon.pacwan.net. Owners: Madame Marie-France Mille and Monsieur François Mille (page 84).

OUSTAU DE BAUMANIÈRE, Les Baux, 13520 Les Baux de Provence. Tel: (0) 490 97 33 07; FAX: (0) 490 54 40 46. E-mail: oustau@relaischateaux.fr. Owner and chef: Jean-André Charial (page 146).

LAVENDER TRAILS

COTTA, ANNY. LE COLOMBIER, Route de Moustiers, 04410 Puimoisson. Tel: (0) 492 74 54 26. Producer of lavandin, distillery.

FERME ST. AGRICOLE, 84390 Savoillans. Tel: (0) 475 28 86 57; FAX: (0) 475 28 86 62. Aromatherapy, food, botanic gardens.

JARDINS DES LAVANDES, CATHERINE ET JEAN CLAUDE COUTTOLENC, 84390 Sault. Tel: and FAX: (0) 490 64 14 97. Boutique in town: (0) 490 64 10 74. Nursery.

L'ASSOCIATION DES ROUTES DE LA LAVANDE, Mme. Elizabeth Hauwuy. Tel: (0) 475 26 65 90; FAX: (0) 475 26 32 67. B.P. 36, 26110 Nyons. E-mail: routes.lavande@educagre.fr.

LA BONNE ETAPE, Chemin du Lac, 04160 Château Arnoux. Owner and chef: Jany Gleize. Tel: (0) 492 64 00 09; FAX: (0) 492 64 37 37. E-mail: bonneetape@relaischateaux.fr.

LAVANDE 1100, 84400 Lagarde d'Apt. Tel: (0) 490 75 01 42; FAX: (0) 490 75 01 42. Maurice Fra and family.

PRIEURÉ DE SALAGON, 04300 Mane. Owned by the Conseil général. Tel: (0) 492 75 19 93; FAX: (0) 492 75 25 14. E-mail: salagon@karatel.fr. Fine historic garden.

LOCAL CRAFTS

MAGNAN, JEAN-PIERRE, 8b, rue de Mazeau, 84100 Orange. Tel: (0) 490 34 25 62. Situated in back of the municipal museum in Orange, with a separate entrance. The antiques shop is open 8 A.M. to 12 P.M. and 2 P.M. to 7 P.M. and Saturday mornings. To visit the furniture and instrument workshops, an appointment is necessary (page 150).

MAS DE CUREBOURG, Route d'apt 84800 Isle-sur-la-Sorgue. Tel: (0) 490 20 37 85; FAX: (0) 490 20 23 42. Hélène Degrugillier-Dampeine. Open 10 A.M. to 6 P.M. daily, Sunday 10 A.M. to 12 P.M. and 3 P.M. to 6 P.M. (page 97).

LES OLIVADES, Chemin des Indienneurs, 13103 Saint-Etienne-du-Grès. Tel: (0) 490 49 19 19; FAX: (0) 490 49 19 20. Visits by appointment only. E-mail: les-olivades@provence-fabrics.com (page 77).

A. PARODI ET FAMILLE, the shop is on the main street of Mirabel-aux-Baronnies, between Vaison-la-Romaine and Nyons, northeast of Avignon on the D938. Tel: (0) 475 27 12 07. Open: 9:00 A.M. to 12 P.M.; 2:00 P.M. to 6:00 P.M., every day but Sunday (page 72).

PITOT, ANTONY, Quartier de Ponty, R.N. 100, 84200 Goult. Tel: (0) 490 72 22 79. Visits by appointment (page 165).

RAMPAL-PATOU, 71, rue Félix-Pyat, 13300 Salon-de-Provence. Tel: (0) 490 56 07 28; FAX: (0) 490 56 52 18. Owner: Monsieur R. Rampal (page 40).

LA SCOURTINERIE, 36, la Maladrerie, 26110 Nyons. Tel: (0) 475 26 33 52; FAX: (0) 475 26 20 72. Owner: Monsieur J. Fert. Visits by appointment (page 127).

VERNIN, FABRIQUE. Les Carreaux d'Apt, Le Pont Julien, R.N. 100, 84480 Bonnieux. Tel: (0) 490 04 63 04; FAX: (0) 490 74 00 47. Visits by appointment (page 116).

LOCAL FLAVORS

CONFISERIES JOUVAUD, rue de l'Evêché, 84200 Carpentras. Tel: (0) 490 63 15 38; FAX: (0) 490 63 21 62. E-mail: jouveauddesserts@avignon.pacwan (page 160).

DAGUIN, ANNE, Le Petit Duc: pâtissiers, fabricants de douceurs. 7 boulevard Victor Hugo, 13210 Saint-Rémy-de-Provence. Tel: and FAX: (0) 490 92 08 31 (page 163).

MANGUIN, JEAN-PIERRE, Ile de la Barthelasse, 84000 Avignon. Tel: (0) 490 82 62 29 and (0) 490 86 56 60. Visits by appointment (page 21).

MUSEUMS AND GALLERIES

APARE, 41, cours Jean Jaurès, 84000 Avignon. Tel: (0) 490 85 51 15; FAX: (0) 490 86 82 19, for outdoor terraces (page 32).

CAMARGUE MUSEUM, Mas du Pont de Rousty, 13200 Arles. Tel: (0) 490 97 10 82. Nine miles southwest of Arles on the road to Saintes Maries de la Mer. Open all year except January 1, May 1, and December 25, and Tuesdays in winter (page 42).

FONDATION ANGLADON-DUBRUJEAUD, 5 rue Laboureur, 84000 Avignon. Tel: (0) 490 82 29 03; FAX: (0) 490 85 78 07. Curator: Madame Anne Marie Peylhard. Open afternoons 1 P.M. to 6 P.M. except Mondays and Tuesdays (page 25).

GALERIE LESTRANGER ET COMPTOIR DE LESTRANGER, Place Jean de Renaud, 13210 Saint-Rémy-de-Provence. Tel: (0) 490 92 57 14; FAX: (0) 490 92 69 17. Owner: Catherine Binda-Sterling. E-mail: cst@lestranger.fr. Web: www.lestranger.fr. By appointment only (page 116).

MAS DE LA PYRAMIDE, quartier Saint-Paul, 13210 Saint-Rémy-de-Provence. Tel: (0) 490 92 00 81. Open in summer 9 A.M. to 12 P.M., 2 P.M. to 7 P.M. In winter 9 A.M. to 12 P.M., 2 P.M. to 5 P.M. Owner: Monsieur Mauron. On the D5 leaving the center of Saint-Rémy towards Les Baux (page 64).

MUSÉE DE L'ART CULINAIRE—FONDATION AUGUSTE ESCOFFIER—INSTITUT JOSEPH DONON, 06270 Villeneuve-Loubet (Village). Tel: (0) 493 20 80 51; FAX: (0) 493 73 93 79. Open from 2 P.M. to 6 P.M. summers every day but Monday and holidays. Closed in November (page 167).

MUSEUM OF PROVENÇAL COSTUMES AND JEWELS, Hôtel de Clapiers Cabris, 2, rue Jean Ossola, 06130 Grasse. Tel: (0) 493 36 44 65; FAX: (0) 493 36 03 50 (page 60).

WINE

CAVE DES COTEAUX, 84200 Cairanne. Tel: (0) 490 30 82 05; FAX: (0) 490 30 74 03 (page 130).

CHARTREUSE DE BONPAS, 84510 Caumont. Southeast of Avignon. Tel: (0) 490 23 09 59; FAX: (0) 490 23 19 97. Private property of Monsieur and Madame Casalis. Wine tasting is possible (page 98).

CHÂTEAU D'AQUÉRIA, 30126 Tavel. Tel: (0) 466 50 04 56; FAX: (0) 466 50 18 46. Owner: Monsieur Paul de Bez (page 63).

CHÂTEAU DE MONT-REDON, 84230 Châteauneuf-du-Pape. Tel: (0) 490 83 72 75; FAX: (0) 490 83 77 20. Owners: Messieurs Jean and François Abeille, and Monsieur Fabre (page 47).

COULON, PAUL ET FILS, Domaine de Beaurenard, 84230 Châteauneuf-du-Pape. Tel: (0) 490 83 71 79; FAX: (0) 490 83 71 79 (page 47).

MAISON DU VIN, 6, rue des Trois Faucons, 84024 Avignon. Tel: (0) 490 27 24 14; FAX: (0) 490 27 24 13. E-mail: promo@vivarhone.com. Web: www. vins-rhone.com (page 105).

UNIVERSITÉ DU VIN, Le Château, 26790 Suze-la-Rousse. Tel: (0) 475 97 21 30; FAX: (0) 475 98 24 20. E-mail:université.du.vin@wanadoo.fr (page 102).

Index